how to get more done

Seven days to achieving more

Fergus O'Connell

PEARSON

Prentice Hall

LIFE

Harlow, England • London • New York • Boston • San Francisco • Toronto
Sydney • Tokyo • Singapore • Hong Kong • Seoul • Taipei • New Delhi
Cape Town • Madrid • Mexico City • Amsterdam • Munich • Paris • Milan

PEARSON EDUCATION LIMITED

Edinburgh Gate
Harlow CM20 2JE
Tel: +44 (0)1279 623623
Fax: +44 (0)1279 431059
Website: www.pearsoned.co.uk

First published in Great Britain in 2008

© Pearson Education Limited 2008

ISBN: 978-0-273-71424-8

British Library Cataloguing-in-Publication Data
A catalogue record for this book is available from the British Library

Library of Congress Cataloging-in-Publication Data
O'Connell, Fergus.
   How to get more done : seven days to achieving more / Fergus O'Connell.
      p. cm.
   Includes bibliograpical references and index.
   ISBN 978-0-273-71424-8
   1.   Time management. 2. Achievement motivation. 3. Success. I. Title
   HD69.T54025 2008
   650.1'1--dc22

                                                    2007042501

10 9 8 7 6 5 4 3 2 1
11 10 09 08 07

Typeset in 10/14 Plantin by 30
Printed and bound in Great Britain by Henry Ling Ltd, Dorchester, Dorset

The publisher's policy is to use paper manufactured from sustainable forests.

how to get more done

Prentice Hall LIFE

If life is what you make it, then making it better starts here.

What we learn today can change our lives tomorrow. It can change our goals or change our minds; open up new opportunities or simply inspire us to make a difference. That's why we have created a new breed of books that do more to help you make more of *your* life.

Whether you want more confidence or less stress, a new skill or a different perspective, we've designed *Prentice Hall Life* books to help you to make a change for the better. Together with our authors we share a commitment to bring you the brightest ideas and best ways to manage your life, work and wealth.

In these pages we hope you'll find the ideas you need for the life you want. Go on, help yourself.

It's what you make it

* * *

For Ferga – beautiful, good company, great travelling companion

Contents

About the author

Fergus O'Connell is one of the world's leading authorities on project management and getting things done in the shortest possible time. *The Sunday Business Post* has described him as having 'more strings to his bow than a Stradivarius'. He has a First in Mathematical Physics and has worked in information technology, software development and general management.

Fergus has spent much of the last 30 years either doing, teaching, learning, writing or thinking about project management. In 1992, he founded ETP (www.etpint.com), which is now one of the world's leading programme and project management companies. His project management method – Structured Project Management/ The Ten Steps – has influenced a generation of project managers. In 2003 this method was used to plan and execute the Special Olympics World Games 2003, the world's biggest sporting event that year. His radical methods for shortening projects are in use by a growing band of devotees. His experience covers projects around the world; he has taught project management in Europe, North America, South America and the Far East.

Fergus is the author of seven books, both fiction and non-fiction:

- *How to Run Successful Projects – The Silver Bullet,* 3rd edition (2001);
- *How to Run Successful High-Tech Project-Based Organizations* (1999);

- *How to Run Successful Projects in Web-Time* (2000);
- *Simply Brilliant – The Competitive Advantage of Common Sense*, 2nd edition (2004);
- *Call the Swallow* (2002);
- *How to Do a Great Job – and Go Home on Time* (2005);
- *Fast Projects: Project Management When Time Is Short* (2007).

The first of these, sometimes known simply as 'The Silver Bullet', has become both a bestseller and a classic. *Simply Brilliant* – also a bestseller – was runner-up in the W. H. Smith Book Awards 2002. *Call The Swallow* was short listed for the 2002 Kerry Ingredients Irish Fiction Prize and nominated for the Hughes & Hughes/ Sunday Independent Novel of the Year. His books have been translated into 12 languages.

Fergus has written on project management for *The Sunday Business Post, Computer Weekly* and *The Wall Street Journal*. He has lectured on project management at University College Cork, Trinity College Dublin, Bentley College, Boston University, the Michael Smurfit Graduate School of Business and on television for the National Technological University.

He has two children and lives with his partner in France.

Preface

Thank you for buying this book and welcome to *How to Get More Done*. If you find that:

- you seem to be busy all the time – either at work or in your personal life or both;
- you don't seem to have any time for you;
- you never seem to get free or 'down' time;
- you're not getting to spend time on the things that are really important to you;

then the book will make a real difference to you.

If you do the things which this book describes you will find that:

- you get a lot more done – and I mean a *lot* more;
- a whole heap of your time will free up and become available to you;
- you will spend a great deal more time doing the things that are important to you.

This book is not really a time-management book whose aim is to turn you into a productivity machine. Maybe you know or have tried such books. They teach you a 'system'; you implement the system and soon you are getting great swathes of stuff done. The only problem, of course, is that these swathes of stuff get replaced by – yes, you've guessed it – more swathes of stuff.

No, this book takes a different approach. It takes the view that at any given time each of us has a pile of stuff labelled: 'Have to do/want to do/would like to do'. For most people the total amount of work involved if they were to do all of these things is significantly – i.e. it could be many, many times – greater than the amount of time available to do them.

You need to do less but achieve more. This book shows you how to do exactly that.

Therefore, you don't need time management, at least not in the conventional sense. What you need is something far more radical than that. *You need not to do a whole pile of things.* You need to do less but achieve more. This book shows you how to do exactly that.

If you want to 'get more done', then you are going to have to change your behaviour. This book tries to get you to do that over seven days. During that time it essentially tries to get you to engage in three new behaviours. They are:

- not doing stuff;
- only doing the right stuff;
- doing as little as possible when doing the right stuff.

This book is the teacher. All it requires is that you be at a place in your life where you are ready to learn and to change some things.

The book is organised into seven parts, one for each of seven days. Each day has very specific things it asks you to do and specific targets that you have to achieve for that day. You can do the seven days sequentially or not as you choose. If you fail to achieve a particular day's targets, you can just keep at it until you achieve them. If it all goes to hell, you can start again at Day 1. There is a Zen proverb that goes, 'When the pupil is ready to learn, a teacher will appear.' This book is the teacher. All it requires is that you be at a place in your life where you are ready to learn and to change some things.

How do you know if you're at such a place? While the signs can be different for different people, there are some common ones. A vague dissatisfaction with things. A feeling that you can't go on doing what you're doing – that it's all too much and the time has come for a change. Sleeplessness, irritability, too many sick-days. A feeling that 'there must be more to life than this'. Fear of making a change. Finding excuses not to make a change – that the time is not right, or your financial situation won't allow it. These are some of the signs that you need to look at what you do and make some changes.

The seven-day programme starts off gently. Day 1 is about making some preparations for the journey you are about to undertake. It gets you to analyse your own situation and gives some insights into them. Day 2 gets you to put together the 'system' you will need to get more done and to identify what's important to you. The next three days cover the three new behaviours – how to not do stuff (day 3), how to do the right stuff (day 4), and how to do as little as possible (day 5). Day 6 gives you some more ideas about planning for the unplanned, being flexible and creating extra time in your day. Day 7 is where you have to put it all together and commit to what you're going to do.

I illustrate a lot of the ideas with examples from my own experience. I hope you'll understand and sympathise with why I do this. It's not that I'm the most incredibly interesting guy you're likely to meet. Nor is it that the specific problems which I describe and which are unique to me, are so completely fascinating. Rather it is this. The problems I describe in this book – issues like not having enough time or spending time in the right places – are, I believe, pretty much universal. I can speak authoritatively on my own situation; about what actions I have taken, what has worked and what hasn't, the difficulties and fears I have faced, and sometimes overcome. I hope that in doing this you will see how one ordinary person has applied them and made a difference, and that you too can use them to change the way you live your life.

I teach courses in how to get more done. The courses give participants an extensive 'menu' of ideas from which to choose. (This book does exactly the same thing.) There is a point in the course where each person has to say what they're going to do going forward. One of the things that never ceases to amaze me is how no two people decide to do the same things. It shows why time-management 'systems' (courses/books/CDs/DVDs) have such limited effect. These systems are a one-size-fits-all solution. They work brilliantly for some people; they give others some temporary improvement and they leave some people cold. (In that respect they're a bit like diets!)

You shouldn't be surprised by this. To change your behaviour, you need some spark to ignite something in you. Only then will you start to do something differently. It seems to me that if you get a large enough menu of things to try – which is what you get with this book – you're far more likely to find something that will tickle your fancy, resonate with you and set you off on a new road.

I'd like to know if you found the book useful or if it made any kind of difference. Or not! With that in mind you can e-mail me at fergus.oconnell@etpint.com with any brickbats or bouquets (or anything in between).

Acknowledgements

The biggest thank you must go to all of the people who've attended my courses on this subject over the years and from whom I've learned so much.

Thanks once again to my editor, Samantha Jackson, for all her energy and passion for the book.

Finally, a big debt of gratitude to Clare and Val on whose computers I finished this book when my own hard disk packed up the week the manuscript was meant to be delivered. A close run thing!

Introduction

don't know much about dying – not having done it yet – but I do know this: when I die there will be a whole bunch of things that I won't have done. Maybe I'll regret them, maybe I won't, but there is no doubt that they won't have been done. My guess is that when the time comes, everybody is going to be like this. There are going to be whole lists of things that they haven't done.

The central idea of *How to Get More Done* – the way you're going to get more done – *is by not doing certain things*. I'll write that again just in case you feel you didn't read it correctly. The way you're going to get more done is by not doing certain things. You're either:

● not going to do them at all; or

● postpone them for as long as possible; or

● when you do have to do them, do the least amount of work necessary to get the job done.

There's a popular time-management book that talks about the 'two-minute rule'. The idea of the two-minute rule is that if you can get something done in less than two minutes, then you do it. I often imagine the epitaph, carved on the gravestone of the man who followed the two-minute rule. It goes, 'Here lies Charlie – he got all the small things done'.

I often imagine the epitaph, carved on the gravestone of the man who followed the two-minute rule. It goes, 'Here lies Charlie – he got all the small things done'.

You don't want to get the small things done. You want to get the big things done. And by big things, I don't mean big in terms of how much work they'll take. I mean *big* in terms of how important they are to you in your life. If you get these things done, then you will truly feel that you are getting more done.

But isn't this just a time-management problem?

Well, if it is, a time-management book will solve it. There are plenty of them out there. On the day I typed in 'time management' to amazon (.co.uk) I was astonished to get 2,704 results. These books appear to be of two types. There are what you might call technical time-management books, full of tips such as the two-minute rule mentioned above, and there are how-to-live-the-life-you-were-meant-to-live kind of books. Somebody once described them to me as 'outward-looking' and 'inward-looking' time-management approaches and I think, in some ways, this is a good description.

The technical ones – the outward-looking ones – give you a 'system' and, provided you follow that system, your life will be more organised. Such systems suit some people very well. These people like going on a course and coming back with the snazzy looking binder and different forms for everything you could possibly imagine. Or they like the feeling when they buy lots of folders and coloured pens and other items of stationery and then create their new system and put it to work. For the people who like to work this way, such books and methods can be truly life-changing.

But for many people these systems don't work. I think it's because while some people like to work in this way, many people don't. For many people these systems are too regimented. Many people don't like the notion that they'll have an item somewhere in their 'system' that reads 'have informal "how are you?" conversation with my PA'. Or even worse, such items about their home life – 'plan holiday with wife and kids'. So they often buy the multi-coloured stationery and end up giving it to their children to use as colouring books.

You need a system alright, but you need a *flexible* system, one that suits the way you like to work. You also, I think, need your system to be forgiving, so that if you let things lapse for a while, your system won't fall apart and then, when you start to apply yourself again, the system should come back into action pretty quickly.

> We'd all like to go on a two-week residential workshop in the Bahamas where we could check out of the world and contemplate our lives, but for most of us that isn't going to happen any time soon.

As for the how-to-live-the-life-you-were-meant-to-live books – the inward-looking time-management books – well, there's an expression that goes, 'It's hard to drain the swamp when you're up to your neck in alligators'. Yes, we'd all like to go on a two-week residential workshop in the Bahamas where we could check out of the world and contemplate our lives, but for most of us that isn't going to happen any time soon. And if you buy a how-to-live-the-life-you-were-meant-to-live book, the chances are that you'll end up reading it a few pages a night, before you drop off to sleep exhausted. Is it going to change your life? Probably not.

I assume you are like most people:

- There is stuff you have to do – some you do because you have to; some because you like to.
- There is stuff you would do more of, if you got the chance.
- There is stuff you would do less of, if you got the chance.
- There is some stuff you'd rather not do at all.

This book is about doing more of the stuff you have to do and want to do and less of the other stuff – if that's not too many 'stuffs'.

So how is the reprogramming going to be done?

To answer this question, you need to know about Dilt's Neurological Levels of Change.[1]

Dilt's Neurological Levels of Change, developed by Californian psychologist, Robert Dilts, is a useful way of thinking about behavioural change. It can be illustrated as shown in the diagram.

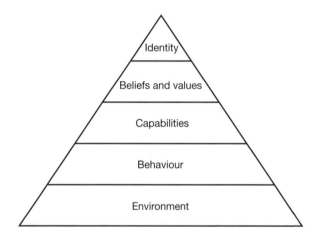

Dilt's Neurological Levels of Change

The levels are explained like this:

Identity

Who are you? Identity gives you your basic sense of self and your core values. Identity has primarily to do with your mission in life. It is the deepest (or highest) level.

Beliefs and values

This level has to do with your values and beliefs. It answers the question: why am I doing this? Beliefs and values are the various ideas you think are true and use as a basis for daily action. Beliefs can be both enabling/releasing and limiting.

Capabilities

This level describes what you are capable of – how you deal with things. It covers the sets of behaviours, mental models, general skills and strategies that you use in your life.

Behaviours

Behaviours consist of the specific actions or reactions you take within your daily environment. Regardless of your capabilities, behaviour describes what you actually do.

Environment

This is about the external context in which behaviour occurs.

According to the model, the levels influence each other in both directions. However, a change on a higher level will have a greater impact on the lower levels than the other way round.

You can see how this goes then for behaviour change in the time-management arena. You go on a time-management course and learn a new skill (Capability). However, if the organisation you work for sees itself (Identity) as a work-all-the-hours-god-sends sort of organisation, then the chances are that its Identity will overwhelm your Capability.

If though, you could change either your beliefs and values or your identity, then the chances are that these changes would be much more likely to remain permanent. That is what you are going to try to do in the chapters that follow. I'm going to try to get you to change some of your beliefs, your values, your *principles*.

Now for many people, myself included, 'principle' is rather a big, intimidating and scary word. It carries with it connotations of codes of belief, rules, laws, axioms, dogma, and that is really not the sense we want here. Rather than rules let's think in terms of signs – those big road signs, for example, that you see on motorways/freeways/*autoroutes*. They're the signs in blue and white (or green and white in the USA) that are just impossible to ignore as they are so big. With road signs like this, when you are faced with a decision about which way to go, the sign should nudge you in the right direction.

This is also what you want from your principles. They should nudge you in the right direction. If they do, then every time you go in that direction, the principle should result in a new behaviour. If you take this new direction and engage in this new behaviour often enough, the new behaviour will become a habit. And then you will have your 'system', but you will have it painlessly, effortlessly and in a way that works for you. It will also be a system that is likely to survive when life gets in the way.

This then, is what you are going to do. You are going to make changes that could be very deep-seated and long-lasting. Turn the page and have a look at what Day 1 involves.

What's the problem?

D ay 1 is all about you. It's only through a thorough understanding of you and your situation that you can start to make the right changes in the right way:

'If I can help them to understand their situation better, I may have allowed them to see more clearly what risks and opportunities lie before them.'

Myself and Other More Important Matters, Charles Handy

There are three exercises that will help you achieve this in each of the chapters and they are designed to find out:

1 your behaviours when you try to get things done;

2 where you spend your time at the moment;

3 what you've tried to help you get things done.

It may be that you have a strong foundation of good habits to work with, or it may be that you have to overturn everything you are used to, but, whatever the case, the process of habit breaking needn't be the teeth-gritting battle we often make it out to be – Chapter 4 will show you how!

CHAPTER 1

What are you like?

S o what are you like? How do you work? How do you go about accomplishing things? What things cause roadblocks? I want you to get some insights into the way you work. Later on you'll be able to use these insights to figure out which ideas in this book will work best for you. In this chapter I get you to answer some questions which will provide these insights; in later chapters you will use what you have learned.

> I want you to get some insights into the way you work.

What stops you from getting more done?

Take a look at the following questionnaire and score each of the statements on a scale of 1–5 where:

1 = Strongly disagree

2 = Disagree

3 = Feel neutral

4 = Agree

5 = Strongly agree.

Later on I'll get you to look at those statements where you scored 5. For each of these I'll point at the precise solution to that cause.

I'm stopped from getting more done because:	1 = Strongly disagree	2 = Disagree	3 = Feel neutral	4 = Agree	5 = Strongly agree
1. Of inadequate staffing levels/ staffing shortages/staff not being replaced/being under-resourced					
2. Of having an inexperienced team/staff not trained to the required level					
3. I do specialised work which cannot be easily shared					
4. Several of my projects have the same priority level					
5. Of my organisation's inability to say 'no'					

6. Of my inability to say 'no'. I'm the proverbial nice guy/gal and want to help people as much as possible					
7. Of taking on too much work/too many projects					
8. Of misusing of time – not documenting and setting goals with time limits					
9. I'm not really disciplined in the management of my time					
10. I get more work and projects but don't get more resources					
11. Of aggressive timescales within the organisation					

12. I jump from one thing to another without completing the first task				
13. I don't manage projects properly				
14. I accept more work/projects to try to gain more knowledge				
15. Of the pace the organisation works at				
16. I have more work to do than time available to do it				
17. Of teething problems due to something being new, e.g. a new job or department or structure				

18. I over commit to other people				
19. I over commit when I take on new tasks/ projects				
20. I take on new tasks/projects before completing old ones				
21. Of a lack of knowledge of the organisation in which I work				
22. Of difficulties with estimating the work required accurately				
23. Of projects that are regarded as completed by management but still require work				

24. Of not delegating				
25. Of being too ambitious in terms of what I thought I could achieve				
26. Of the culture of the organisation				
27. Of the national culture where I work				
28. Of covering for other people on annual or sick leave				
29. Of something not being done properly or completely so that it has to be done again				

30. Of too many people asking me to do too many things				
31. Of people not knowing what I'm currently doing so they assume I'm not busy				
32. Of multiple things to do				
33. Of moving between jobs and currently having an overlap				
34. Of accepting stuff that is not my job				
35. Of having too many roles				

36. That's just the way I am				
37. I haven't told my boss				
38. I say 'yes' to everything				
39. Of not asking for help				
40. I have a lot of stuff to do				
41. Of not enough time to complete all tasks to a satisfactory level				

42. Of firefighting				
43. Of bad planning				
44. Of wrong estimates				
45. People keep interrupting me so I can't follow my intended plan				
46. People don't do what they learned in training				
47. Of getting small things out of the way so that I can then focus on the bigger ones				

48. Of losing people to other projects				
49. I'm just not very well organised				
50. I deal with emergencies rather than planning				
51. I don't do the most important thing first				
52. I don't like to say 'no'				
53. I don't feel I can say 'no'				

54. Projects never end completely				
55. I always prioritise other peoples' stuff over my own activities				
56. Of not using my time-management system				
57. Of requests coming from upper management				
58. People don't check on my availability				
59. Not enough time is given to planning				

60. I haven't implemented time-management training with sufficient discipline. I implemented it but then went back to my old ways

61. I have not always prioritised the most important jobs

62. Of constant change/demands on my time

63. Of not always appreciating the scale of what I've been asked to do. By the time I do, commitments have already been made and have to be delivered on

64. People are not always available to help

65. Of the nature of the business – things constantly change and I have to adapt

66. There is no one else to do it				
67. Management don't account for my current workload before giving me more work				

CHAPTER 2

Where are you spending your time at the moment?

f you can't measure it, you can't manage it', the old saw goes. Therefore, you need to figure out where you're spending your time at the moment. You can do this for just your work life or your life as a whole. I do it for your work life first to show you how it's done. After that you can do it for your whole life.

Here's what you do:

Figure out everything you have to do

1 Pick a period of time – a month, a couple of months, from now to the end of next month, from now to the end of the quarter, half a year, the rest of the year – whatever suits you.

2 Make a list of all the projects you will be working on during the period that you've chosen. Include on the list any project which:

- ends during the period that you've chosen;
- starts during the period you've chosen;
- starts and ends in the period you've chosen;
- runs through the period that you've chosen.

3 Now add to the list what might be called 'business as usual' or 'day-job' type things. These would be things like:

- Meetings. All your meetings may be about particular projects, but most of us have things like 'the group

meeting', 'the Monday meeting', 'company meeting' and so
on. Don't forget too that you may have to do preparation
before a meeting, there will be the meeting itself and you
may have to do follow-ups or action items afterwards.

- Reports. Maybe your job involves producing (or reading) a
lot of these.

- Interruptions. Whether they come person-to-person or
by phone (landline or mobile), every one of us has these
every day.

- Inbox/e-mail. Possibly all of your e-mails are related to
specific projects, but most of us have other stuff we have to
deal with every day. And anyway, there's the time involved in
figuring out whether they're about specific projects or not.

- Trips/visits. Maybe you're going on a business-related trip
or somebody's coming to visit you and that will soak up
your time.

- Training. Maybe you're being trained on some form of
training course or you're training somebody else.

- Annual leave/vacation/holidays. Always nice!

- Managing people. Maybe you're the line manager of some
bunch of people and this takes up your time.

- Phone calls. We all have some/a lot of these to deal with
every day.

- Recruitment. Maybe your organisation is expanding and
you have to spend time looking at résumés, interviewing
people and doing related activities.

- Firefighting. Speaks for itself!

- Filling in for people. Maybe you're standing in for people
who are away on some kind of leave.

4   Add an additional line item called, 'New stuff'. It may be that
in your job nothing is going to change over the period that
you're looking at. (I've heard there are jobs like that though
I've never come across one myself!) Presumably, what's more
likely is that new things will come along. We don't know what

they are yet because they haven't come along – we just know it's inevitable that they will. 'New stuff' is to cover these.

5   Finally, is there anything else in work that you need to consider? Is there anything that you haven't done that is playing on your mind? Get it out of your head now and down on paper.

Figure out how much time it will take to do it

Now figure out how much of your time is going to go into each of the items on your list over the period that you're looking at. Use hours per day, days per week, total hours, total days or whatever measure seems most appropriate to each line item. Be sure to record each of the amounts of time in the same units. I find days are best for this.

Add all of these up. This gives you the total amount of work you have to do in the period in question.

Figure out how much time you have available

Now figure out how many work days there are in the same period. (Convert that number to hours if you've been using hours in the previous section.) This is how much time you have available.

Dance cards

On my courses, I usually get people to lay out these calculations in what I term a '**dance card**'. The dance card is a reference to those more genteel times where, when women went to dances, they were given a card with a list of the songs that the band/orchestra was going to play. Then, if a gentleman

The dance card was a booking system. If you are overloaded, i.e. if there is more work to do than time available to do it, then one way to think about the problem is that you've gone and overbooked yourself.

wanted to dance with a particular lady, he wrote his name against a particular song on the dance card.

The dance card was a booking system. If you are overloaded, i.e. if there is more work to do than time available to do it, then one way to think about the problem is that you've gone and overbooked yourself.

Examples of dance cards

Here are a couple of examples of dance cards. The chart below contains an example of a dance card for a six-month period. (The calculations assume 20 days in a month and four weeks in a month.)

	120		20	20	20	20	20	20
Job	**Needs**		**Jan**	**Feb**	**Mar**	**Apr**	**May**	**Jun**
Project A	72 days		12	12	12	12	12	12
Project B	24 days		8	8	4	4		
Project C	10 days					2	4	4
Selling	2 dpw		8	8	8	8	8	8
E-mail/Inbox/Admin	1¼ dpw		5	5	5	5	5	5
Holidays	10 days							10
Total work to do	194		33	33	29	31	29	39

Dance card example 1

The column headed 'Job' lists all of the things that the owner of the dance card is involved in. The next column indicates how much work is estimated to go into these things over the period under investigation. Days per month (dpm), days per week (dpw), hours per day or just plain days are all good ways of calculating how much work needs to be done. Then the remaining columns show how this time will be spread out over the period under investigation – in this case, six months.

There are two other items of interest. The top row shows how many days are available per month. The total of these is 120. (Note that rather than trying to allow for the different numbers of working days in different countries, I have assumed that every month consists of 20 days. You could adjust this up or down for your own situation. For example, in Europe, December is definitely not 20 working days in most companies.) The other item of interest is the total of all the work this dance-card owner has to do – in this example, 194 days. In the example then, the owner of this dance card has an overload of more than 50%, i.e. over 50% more work to do than time available to do it.

Dance card example 1 was for a person who does a mixture of projects – which take reasonably predictable amounts of time – and other kinds of work. However, dance cards can also be used by anybody – even if your work is very unpredictable. If your job is like that, then the best thing to do is to record what actually happens, say, in a particular week or over several weeks, and use this as your start point. Dance card example 2 (on page 32) shows one for such a job, with actual time spent in a given week. This one was put together using Excel, but you can do dance cards using anything you like. A piece of paper – as shown in Dance card example 1 – is absolutely fine.

Often, when people do a dance card for the first time, they are surprised. They are surprised by how much they have to do. They are sometimes taken aback by the level of overload they have – how little time available, how much to do. But often too, they find that the dance card explains why they have been spending so long at work, thinking about work or bringing work home with them.

If your dance card is out of balance, i.e. if what you have to do is greater than the time available to do it, then there are only four things you can do. They are:

No.		Total hours	Mon	Tue	Wed	Thu	Fri	Sat	Sun
			8	8	8	8	8	8	0	40
1	Phone calls	9.25	2.25	2.50	3.00	1.00	1.00	0.50	0.00
2	Admin.	7.50	1.75	0.50	0.75	1.50	3.00	0.00
3	Status report to boss	1.00					1.00	
4	Running office	4.75	1.00	0.50	1.00	1.00	1.25	0.00
5	Overseeing staff	6.25	2.00	1.00	1.00	1.25	1.00	0.00
6	E-mail; timesheets; petty cash; stock; phone	5.25	1.00	1.25	0.75	0.75	1.50	0.00
7	Interruptions	7.50	1.00	0.50	2.50	2.00	1.50	0.00
8	Meeting	6.25	0.00	0.75	1.50	3.00	1.00	0.00
9	Bringing work home	6.00		3.00				0.00	3.00
		53.75	9.00	10.00	10.50	10.50	10.75	0.00	3.00

OVERLOAD 34%

Dance card example 2

- You can not do certain things.
- You can not do certain things in the period that you're looking at, i.e. move them off into the future.
- Delegate things or work more hours.
- Reduce the quality of the work you do. (Sometimes people consciously decide to do this; sometimes it just happens.)

Finally, when people find that their dance card is out of balance, they often have a tendency to think the following. They think: 'I'm overloaded at the moment, but once I clear the overload I'll be OK.' Usually, this is not the case. If the dance card is a booking system, then most of us – as long we continue in the jobs we're in – have 'bookings' way off into the future. The person represented in Dance card 1, for example, would appear to have 'bookings' for 'Selling' and 'E-mail/Inbox/Admin' way off into the future. Based on Dance card 1, these 'bookings' amount to $3\frac{1}{4}$ days per week, so they have less then two days per week to devote to project work. Most people are very surprised when they realise this.

Doing a dance card for your whole life

You can also make a dance card for your whole life. To do that, do the following:

1 Pick a period of time – a month, a couple of months, from now to the end of next month, from now to the end of the quarter, half a year, the rest of the year – whatever suits you.

2 Make a list of all the factors in your life. Another way to think about this is to list all the roles you have. Dance card for whole life on page 34 shows an example of this.

There may also be roles that you don't have but that you'd like to have. You've always wanted to be a circus trapeze artist or a concert pianist, for example. Include this in your list of roles.

	Total time available in 6 weeks @ 16 hpd = 672 hours	Work (in hours)	Feb 18	Feb 25	Mar 4	Mar 11	Mar 18	Mar 25
1	Editor bimonthly magazine	16						
2	Director meetings 2 hpw	12						
3	Day job: • Commuting 15 hpw • 8:00 – 3:00/4:30 (35 hours) • Reading ($\frac{1}{2}$ dpw) • 2 x conferences	90 210 24 16						
4	Mother (10 hpw) Daughter – swimming, homework, etc.	60						
5	House (3 hpd, 7 dpw) Cooking, cleaning, ironing, etc.	126						
6	Projects: House rennovation (8 hpw) Holiday planning Learning to tango (2 hpw)	48 4 12						
7	Family/husband (2 hpd)	84						
8	Social life/friends (6 hpw)	36						
9	Dogwalker (1 hpd weekdays)	30						
10	Time for me/Downtime (2 hpd)	84						
	TOTAL	876						

Dance card for whole life

There may also be things that you have been putting off doing – that tax return, that tricky piece of DIY, that difficult phone call you have to make. Add them to your list – if you like under the heading 'Procrastinator'!

3 Now figure out how much of your time is going to go into each of the items on your list over the period that you're looking at. Use hours per day, days per week, total, hours, total days or

whatever measure seems most appropriate to each line item. In this case it's probably best to convert all of these to hours since you are not going to be limited here by the eight hours per day of the normal working day.

4   Notice in the Dance card for whole life that 35 hours per week is the amount listed for the day job. A work-only dance card could confirm whether that was true or not.

5   Add all of these up. This gives you the total amount of work you have to do in the period in question.

6   Now figure out how many hours there are in the same period. (In the Dance card for whole life I have assumed 16 waking hours per day.) This is how much time you have available.

7   The difference between the total in 5 and the total in 6 gives you an overload – if there is one.

Where you're spending your time

Just as with a work-only Dance card, a whole-life dance card can give you some surprising insights. It can explain, for example, why you're run off your feet. More usefully, it can point you to where you might be able to begin thinking about making changes. It can get you to start thinking about priorities – what's important and what's not. And it can get you to consider where hard choices might have to be made. For example, tinkering with the small amounts of time – the 4 or 12 or 16 hours – isn't going to make a great deal of difference in the dance card above. If this person wants to reduce their overload, they are going to have to target the big amounts of time.

> Just as with a work-only dance card, a whole-life dance card can give you some surprising insights.

Doing a whole-life Dance card will give you similar insights – maybe surprising ones – into where you're spending your time. Maybe everything is as you want it to be – or maybe not. If not then read on.

What if you don't like what you see?

It's possible that you don't like what you see. You have too many things to do. Or too many of the wrong things – things that are not that important to you. And not enough of the things that are important.

So then change it! Imagine how you'd like it to be. Answer these questions, i.e. write down the answers. The questions are in no particular order. Don't worry if there's some overlap between the answers to the questions. The purpose of these questions is to get you thinking about the alternatives to what you're doing at the moment.

1   How would you like things to be? What would be the best possible outcome when you make the changes you're going to make?

2   Who are the other people involved in all of this – people like your boss, your spouse or partner, your children, your customers?

3   How would those people be affected if things were to change? What would it mean to them?

4   Would each of them have to buy-in to the change? (Go through them in turn and say whether they would or not. Also say whether getting them to buy-in would be a problem or not.)

5   Why would they want to buy into it? Go through each of them in turn.

6   Why do you want things to change?

7   Imagine life when you have made this transition. What would a typical day/typical week be like? Write down the answers. Be as specific as you can. What will you do? What will be your routine? Who will you be with or be meeting? Where will you be?

8   Think of each of the people you identified in the answer to question 2 above. If you make this change, what will they be saying about you?

9 How will you feel?

10 Will you have changed as a person? If so, how?

11 What will be your ambitions / hopes / dreams once you've accomplished this change?

12 Will your standard of living have changed? Is this a good thing or a bad thing?

13 Will your view of yourself have changed? If so, how?

14 Do you think it would be difficult to accomplish this change?

15 Would it be worth doing?

16 Could it fail?

17 How would you feel if it did? What would you do?

Visualisation

What you did just now was a technique known as visualisation. It's very powerful. In it you try to picture, in as much detail as possible, the result that you want. You try to experience, to 'feel' the end result.

The boxer Muhammad Ali used to use it. He called it 'future history'. When Ali had agreed to fight somebody, he would run through the fight in his imagination right up to the moment when he had won. He would then freeze the winning mental image and become aware of all his senses as if he were there at that very moment. This is what he called a future history. Although a vision of the future, he had experienced it in such detail that subconsciously he believed it had already happened.

You can use it on quite ordinary things – a meeting for instance. Try to visualise the result that you want; how you will feel walking out of the meeting having gained the outcome you desired. (A friend of mine does

> Try to visualise the result that you want; how you will feel walking out of the meeting having gained the outcome you desired.

this by writing the minutes of a meeting *before* the meeting. Try it some time!)

Or you can use it on a day in work – what do you absolutely intend to achieve today? Or if you've got into the habit of letting weekends slip away not having done very much, you can use this technique to change all that. How would you like things to be on Sunday night when the weekend comes to an end? How would you like to be feeling? How about the other people in your life? Partners? Children?

And then there are the things you don't want to do – that tax return, that tricky piece of DIY, the difficult phone call you have to make. Visualising how you will feel when the thing is done is a fantastic way to get you focused and motivated.

In a perfect world somebody would pay you to go on a two-week retreat (in an exotic location, naturally) where you would have time to ponder these big questions about where your life is going, and how you're spending your time and what you're trying to achieve and what legacy you want to leave. That probably isn't going to happen any time soon. Visualisation is the cheap, realistic and completely effective alternative. It's the budget airline that gets you there just as well as the first-class airfare does. And what's more there are no carbon emissions!

Visualisation versus delusion

It's important to highlight the difference between visualisation and delusional thinking. Muhammad Ali did his future history, sure. But he also *prepared*. He developed skills and techniques. Without these he would have merely been deluding himself.

We too need to develop skills and techniques to support our efforts to change. These are what the rest of the book is all about.

CHAPTER 3

What other things have you tried?

You may have been trying to get more done for some time and it's likely you've tried various techniques to help that haven't made a difference. In finding a solution, it's important that you understand why these techniques haven't helped.

> It's likely you've tried various techniques to help that haven't made a difference.

The questionnaire below will help you determine just that – as with the first questionnaire, we'll be using the scores a little later to find out which ideas in the book will work best for you.

Take a look at the following questionnaire and score each of the statements on a scale of 1–5 where:

1 = Strongly disagree

2 = Disagree

3 = Feel Neutral

4 = Agree

5 = Strongly agree.

I haven't been able to get more done because:	1 = Strongly disagree	2 = Disagree	3 = Feel neutral	4 = Agree	5 = Strongly agree
1. People keep interrupting me so that I can't follow my intended plan					
2. People don't do what they learned in training and keep coming to me for help					

3. I try to get the small things out of the way so that I can focus on the important things; but then I find that I don't have enough time for the important things				
4. Extra resources are not available				
5. I keep losing people to other projects				
6. I feel that I just don't have any choice. This is the hand I've been dealt. I've made my bed, as the saying goes, and so I must lie in it				
7. I keep dealing with emergencies ('firefighting') rather than planning				
8. I don't know how to organise/plan projects properly				

9. Work keeps coming				
10. The more work I complete, the more work comes to me				
11. I don't do the most important things first				
12. Of lack of time to try to get on top of the problem – it's hard to drain the swamp when you're up to your neck in alligators				
13. I don't like to say 'no'				
14. I don't feel I can say 'no'				

15. I just have too many things on the go				
16. I always prioritise things involving other people over stuff I have to do myself				
17. I have a time-management system but I don't use it				
18. Of requests that come from upper management				
19. People don't check on my availability				
20. I don't devote enough time to planning				

21. I haven't implemented my time-management training with sufficient discipline. I implemented it and then went back to my old habits

22. I have not always prioritised the most important jobs

23. Of constant change/demands on my time

24. I don't always appreciate the scale of what I've been asked to do. By the time I do, commitments have already been made and have to be delivered on

25. Of the culture of the organisation

26. Of my own personality/culture. I'm the proverbial nice guy/gal and want to help people as much as possible

27. People are not always available to help				
28. Of the nature of the business – things constantly change and I have to adapt				
29. There is no one else to do it				
30. I can't change my boss				
31. Projects are often last minute				
32. There are no extra resources available				

33. I haven't explained the problem to my boss

34. I haven't tried to address the problem

35. I need to quantify the problem

CHAPTER 4

Changing habits

Habits are at the root of how productive and effective we are. This is why, on your first day, it's so important for you to see what habits you've developed over time. By creating a dance card and filling in the questionnaires you should begin to have a fair idea of what good and bad habits you've developed, and to realise that to get more done some things will need changing.

Without a doubt, changing ingrained habits is difficult, but it is possible with the right mindset.

Changing ingrained habits is difficult, but it is possible with the right mindset.

The power of the imagination

Do the following. Using, say, the bottom of a glass or something like that, draw a circle on a sheet of paper. Then put a cross through it as shown.

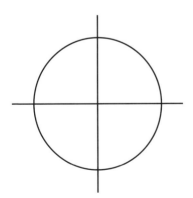

Now tie some object like a heavy ring or a key onto a piece of string about 15 centimetres long. Hold the string with the object about three centimetres above the intersection of the cross. Now ignore the object and the string and instead think about the circle. Trace its circumference with your eyes, following it around either clockwise or anti-clockwise.

After a few moments, the pendulum will begin to swing in the direction in which your eyes have been moving. At first it will make a very small circle but this will steadily widen. If you reverse the direction and follow the circle in the other direction, the pendulum will gradually start to move in the other direction. The same will happen if you start to think about the pendulum tracing the vertical line or the horizontal one.

You may say it's a cheap party trick. Perhaps. However, it's also a demonstration of how important the imagination is in any human endeavour. Here's Thoreau on the subject:

If one advances confidently in the direction of his own dreams, and endeavours to live the life which he has imagined, [my underline] he will meet with a success unexpected in common hours.

And here is another philosopher, Goethe, on the same subject:

Until one is committed, there is hesitancy, the chance to draw back, always ineffectiveness. Concerning all acts of initiation and creation, there is one elementary truth the ignorance of which kills countless ideas and splendid plans: that the moment one definitely commits oneself, then providence moves too. All sorts of things occur to help that would never have otherwise occurred. A whole stream of events issue from the decision, raising in one's favour all manner of unforeseen incidents, meetings and material assistance which no man could have dreamed would have come his way. What you can do or dream [my underline], begin it. Boldness has genius, power and magic in it. Begin it now.

Use the imagination

So in the six days which are to follow it's crucial that you embark on this journey with a relaxed state of mind. Picture yourself succeeding in doing the thing I have asked you to do. Picture how each success that you achieve is causing you to do less and achieve more. See how the accumulation of these successes is moving you closer and closer to the day when you will be doing exactly what you want to do.

Try to forget any difficulties you run into or setbacks you have. Don't dwell on these. Instead hold the dream of the future you're trying to make for yourself.

What's the system?

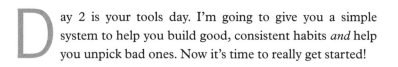

ay 2 is your tools day. I'm going to give you a simple system to help you build good, consistent habits *and* help you unpick bad ones. Now it's time to really get started!

CHAPTER 5

The system

You're going to need some kind of system if you're going to get more done. This is what most time-management books spend the majority of their time talking about. Yet, different systems work for different people. To try to shoehorn everybody into the one fixed system is going to mean that for many people the system will not work. You want the system I described in the Introduction – flexible, one that encourages rather than hinders, a forgiving system and a system that works for you. So what's the best way to find such a system? Why, make one up for yourself, of course!

This chapter describes the elements of the system you will need. You're going to need four things and they are:

- The list. This is the most important element. The list is where you keep all of the things that are contending to be done.
- A way of tracking appointments.
- A filing system.
- A way of recording where your time goes.

The list

Yesterday you did a dance card and looked at your own situation. It should have given you food for thought. It should also have given you the list. The list is where you are going to store all the things that are contending to be done.

A mental image of the list

I'll talk about how you physically store the list in a moment – it can be done in many different ways. But in your head the mental image you should keep of the list is always the same. It is a long piece of paper with lots of items on it and where each line item is numbered.

The list is constantly changing. New things get added to it, things already on it change and things get completed. As new things come along you find a place for them and (mentally) write them in. If something changes, you just (mentally) take an eraser, rub it out and rewrite it. If something completes, you (mentally) draw a line through it or (mentally) delete it. The numbers on the list indicate priorities and we'll have lots more to say about this later.

You have to maintain and constantly update the list. As well as items on the list changing, priorities can be changing. You can decide to give something a temporary high priority in order to get it done.

The physical list

Many time-management books and systems spend a long time talking about how your list should be physically stored. A paper filing system; a leather-bound, loose-leaf folder with lots of different forms; Outlook or some computer-based diary tool; a Palm Pilot or Blackberry or fancy phone or some other kind of hand-held device. Yawn! Maybe the reason time-management systems spend so much time talking about this subject is that they don't have much else to say!

How you physically maintain the list is completely irrelevant if you're trying to get more done. You do whatever works for you. I keep my list on the back of a page taken from a page-a-day diary for 2005. It's also worth saying that how I implement my list is constantly evolving. I made some changes to it only yesterday. I made them because these changes are going to enable me to focus on something that needs focusing on. Your list is constantly evolving so it shouldn't come as any surprise that how you store it evolves too.

My list is a part work/part whole-life list. If it was a complete whole-life list I would have written things on it like, 'love my partner', 'love my children'

> My list is a part work/part whole-life list.

and so on. You can do that if you like – it's a matter of personal preference, as pretty much all of this is. I don't really feel the need to do that. I'd like to think I'm doing these things anyway – though maybe my partner and children mightn't agree! All that matters is that you have a list.

My list also has another component. You can think of it as a branch off the mainline. Every day I write a list of the stuff I need to get done that day. I do it either first thing in the morning or – and it's much better – last thing the previous day. My list for today happens to be written on an index card that I picked up somewhere. Whatever my list for today is written on – and I'll write it on anything's that's to-hand – it always has three parts to it.

On the left hand side are the things I have to write. On the right hand side are people I have to phone. At the bottom I keep a list of anything else I have to do today. Today there's nothing written in this part. This doesn't actually mean I have nothing to do. In fact, the biggest job I have to do today – the one that's going to take up the bulk of the day – isn't written down at all. Today I have to remove carpet from the house we have just bought and will be moving into shortly. Why is it not written down? Well, it's a bit like the elephant in the room – I'm unlikely to miss it. But if I wanted to write it down just to have the satisfaction of crossing it off, which I sometimes do, then that's OK too.

So that's my list. Does it sound pretty disorganised, clunky, old fashioned? Sure, maybe. But in that case you write your list in whatever way works for you. Just make sure you have a list. That's the important thing.

A way of tracking appointments

Next you need a way of tracking appointments. I used to use a paper diary. Now I use a spreadsheet in Excel. This is just because different people need to know where I am and so I can easily e-mail the Excel spreadsheet to people.

A filing system

There may come a time in the future when the world is paperless. Certainly the people who are supposed to know about things have been predicting it since the mid-eighties. Remember the paperless office? I'm not actually convinced about these predictions myself. Give people cheap and widely available laser printers and photocopiers and what do you think they're going to do with them?

Anyway, that's not my subject today. I'm doing my best to make my world paperless. Just the other day, my mobile operator told me that a year's worth of bills for the average customer takes 100 pages. I promptly cancelled my paper bill and from now on will get it online. But it seems for the moment there will always be paper.

There is current paper and paper that's no longer current and so needs to be filed. Like most people I have a filing system, i.e. paper file folders for the latter stuff. I'm the world's worst person for filing things away. I'd much rather throw stuff out and always have a large bin for the purpose and use it vigorously. But for the stuff that needs to be filed, I have files.

A way of recording where your time goes

In some ways this is the most important of all. If you know where your time is going, and you're not happy with it, you can change it. But first you have to know. I know where my days go because as I explained earlier I record them in the Excel spreadsheet. But I also like to summarise how I spend my time. I do this in a dance card.

And that's it. To recap you need four things:

- a list;
- a way of tracking appointments;
- a filing system;
- a way of recording where your time goes.

They can be all integrated in some wonderful system or gizmo. They can also be as eccentric as the ones I've just described.

Put together your system

So now you need to put together all the elements of your system. Here's the checklist.

The list. You need to have a list of all the things contending to be done. The list can be all integrated in one place or kept in different places. Everything can be on the list or there can be certain things that you regard as so obvious that you don't need to write them down. When new things occur, you can physically add them to the list or mentally add them to the list, i.e. you just regard them as there. Each of us will have only one list but its physical manifestation will be as unique as we are unique. Your list will be represented in whatever form works best for you.

> Each of us will have only one list but its physical manifestation will be as unique as we are unique.

A way of tracking appointments. Paper diary, the latest model of high-tech, hand-held organiser or anything in between. Whatever works best for you.

A filing system. Same remarks apply. A few files in a pile (as I do). I'm not recommending it. It's more an admission than a boast. A bank of filing cabinets neatly and precisely labelled and ordered. Whatever suits the way you work.

A way of recording where your time goes. If you don't have something then I find a spreadsheet is good. Work out a layout that works for you. I summarise the hours I work into weeks and eventually the weeks into months. I analyse the proportion of my time that goes into my key activities. You may say that this is far too much summarising and analysis, but that's OK. It's what I need. It's the analysis that tells me about the things that are important to me. You don't have to do the same. Just whatever suits you. Analyse the factors that give you the answers to the questions you are asking. How much of your time disappears every day in interruptions? How much of your time do you spend answering e-mails? Where does your time actually go every day? Week? Over a month? How much time do you spend working each week? Are you happy with this? How much time do you spend on what you've identified to be your number 1 priority? How much time do you spend with your kids? Your wife or husband or partner? Whatever you're interested in? Once you start measuring it, you can start managing it and making it more the way you want it to be.

Don't do stuff

t's a simple thing to do, so why do so many of us find it so hard to say 'no'? Can you imagine how much more time you would have if only you could bring yourself to say it? Thankfully saying 'no' is a skill and I'm going to teach you how to put this magic word into use. I'm also going to teach you the art of 'letting things go hang' – get ready to find yourself with some time on your hands!!

CHAPTER 6

Learn to say 'no'

I f you are in an overload situation, then one way to look at the problem is that you've just said 'yes' too many times.

You are conditioned to think in terms of saying 'yes'. You get things like contracts, job descriptions, lists of objectives and key performance indicators all telling you what you're expected to do, what you should say 'yes' to. Yet, if you say yes to too many things – a bit like eating too much – you get clogged and become unable to function. Then you can't meet your job description or your objectives. Or you can – but only at the cost of your health or the other areas of your life.

You need to be able to think in terms of saying 'no'. It is a skill just like playing the piano or wind-surfing. It's also just as valid a business skill as knowing how to manage people or read a spreadsheet. You need to practise this skill and get good at it. Then you will only say 'yes' to things that really matter.

> You need to be able to think in terms of saying 'no'. It is a skill just like playing the piano or wind-surfing.

In some ways, the term 'saying "no"' is a bad one. It always carries with it the sense of being obnoxious, inflexible, aggressive, hostile. Yet, it is possible to say 'no' and be none of these things. This chapter lists a whole host of ways. But before that, here's an interesting exercise.

 **exercise**

Presumably you have a job description which you or somebody else has written. Sit down, take a piece of paper and write your 'anti-job description'. If a job description is a list of all things you should do, an anti-job description is a list of all the things you *shouldn't* do. I'm not talking about things like coffee breaks or chatting with people at work that you like, or similar. I mean all of the things that you do that take valuable (irreplaceable) time away from the things that are really important. Give yourself 15 minutes and see what you come up with.

Once you have the list, try to stop doing the things on your anti-job description.

Deflecting things

1   Question why a thing needs to be done in the first place.

2   Deflect *some* requests, i.e. tell your boss you're at saturation point. (See what happens when you do.)

3   Delegate more and let go when you do. (Train the people you delegate to, if necessary, to enable you to do this.) In the home can you find people to do the job for you? For instance, if you tend to do all the chores in the house, maybe you can give some to the kids – even very young ones. Teach a three- or four-year-old to do the vacuuming or the dishes. It'll give them a life skill, senses of responsibility, importance and achievement and what's more, they'll love doing it.

4   Stop saying yes to everything you're given → always negotiate. Look to revise or decline deadlines.

5   Challenge peoples' demands for your time/be miserly with your time/be less tolerant of people wasting your time/charge for your time, i.e. find a way to penalise people for wasting it/don't allow other people to control your time/'I'm in control of my time' –

(a) give them alternatives;

(b) take turns regarding venue;

(c) have appointments rather than drop-ins;

(d) have a proper meeting rather than exchanging a large number of e-mails.

6 Make people aware of consequences, i.e. tell them that 'if I do this, I'm not going to be able to do that' or 'Yes, I can get that done but then this is going to be delayed.'

7 It may be possible for you to do a FAQ (frequently asked questions) or some other form of documentation that will get rid of your most common interruptions.

8 Get people to read the manual ('RTFM').

9 Try not to take jobs from other people (taking the monkey from their back and putting it onto yours). Try to get monkeys off your back.

10 Don't be so helpful.

11 Don't do something that's not in your job description.

12 Redistribute work.

13 Somebody's asked you to do something by a certain date or time. Ask if it would do by a later date or time.

14 Inform them of your workload and ask them to prioritise. A dance card would be an excellent way of doing this.

15 Question what exactly they want.

16 Ask them to fill out 'the form'.

17 See if you can pass the thing on to somebody else.

Getting time for yourself

18 Have quiet time or a so-called 'power hour'. Some people call it 'me time'.

19 Implement red time/green time. To do this you divide the day into red time and green time. You might, for example, say that

10:00–11:30 and 2:30–3:30 are going to be your red time. During red time you can't be disturbed and won't take any kind of interruptions. If somebody tries to interrupt you during red time, you politely explain that the earliest you'll be able to talk to them is when your next green time slot begins. For certain jobs you might have to put an arrangement in place to cover when you're in red time. Also it might be good to explain to those you work with that you're carrying out this system. If nothing else, it might encourage them to do the same.

20 Say, 'I'm really involved in this thing at the moment' – indicating something on your desk – 'Can I come back to you at [beginning of next green time slot]?' Most people will respect something like this. Say it whether it's actually true or, not, i.e. whether you are actually involved in something or not.

21 Speak to your partner/husband/wife/children/housemates/ flatmates if you have a backlog that isn't being cleared or an unmanageable load of stuff to do. Ask them if they can help or, better still, tell them what they could do to help. Get their buy-in/support to actions you're proposing to take.

22 Speak to your boss if you have a backlog that isn't being cleared.

23 Make yourself 'not available' –

    (a)   switch off mobile/set mobile to 'Silent' or 'Meeting';

    (b)   make better use of out-of-office message and voice mail/set phone to 'busy';

    (c)   divert your phone.

24 Work (a day or some block of time) from home.

25 Work from another building/location.

26 Work from another desk/get away from your desk.

27 Work in a place where people aren't expecting to find you.

28 Establish more flexible working arrangements with regard to where/when you work.

29 Establish more flexible working hours. (Shift your working hours forwards or backwards in the day.)

30 Isolate yourself.

31 Book time in your calendar for yourself/set aside time/schedule in your private time/organise a meeting with yourself and treat it the same as any other meeting with other people.

32 Do one thing at a time and don't allow yourself to be interrupted while you're doing it.

Dealing with e-mail

33 Turn off e-mail indicator/stay out of e-mail/no e–mails one day a week/delete all e-mails – if it's urgent they'll send it again/keep a full inbox and just deal with the things that align with your priorities/don't keep checking e-mails – check 2–4 times a day/write better quality e-mails, e.g. always give an action/work from most recent to oldest e-mail.

34 Ignore the email or don't reply. (You know if it's important enough they'll re-send it and you can always say that you never got it, the server must have been down!)

Meetings

35 Reduce the number of meetings and meeting times.

36 Decline meetings.

37 Leave meetings when your bit is finished ('Can I do my bit first?').

38 Always have a proper agenda. An agenda is not just a list of items to be covered. It is a list of items to be covered with times allocated to each.

39 Refuse to go to a meeting that doesn't have an agenda.

40 Start and finish on time.

41 Give people who are late for meetings jobs to do, e.g. write the minutes.

42 Rotate the chairing of meetings.

43 Nobody gets out until the deal is done or the problem sorted.

44 Have a standing meeting.

45 Run more effective meetings, i.e. have rules.

46 Never go to a meeting that has more than, say, three people.

Useful phrases

47 'I'm full.'

48 'I wouldn't be the best person to do that – so-and-so is much more qualified than me.'

49 'I can't do it now, but could do it later.'

50 'No.'

51 'I can't do it, but I can find you somebody who can.'

52 'I'm not going to have time to do a proper job and I'd rather not do it at all than do a poor job.'

53 'You'd do a far better job of that than I would.'

54 'Send me more details.'

55 'I'm really too busy at the moment.'

56 'You're going to have to ask my manager/boss about this.'

57 'The people who prioritise these things will have to decide on your request.'

58 'It's outside our remit.'

59 If somebody's asking you to come to a meeting, say 'Send me an agenda.'

60 'I won't be able to do it today. When do you need it by?'

61 'No, because …'

62 'I'll take a look at it and see what's involved. I can't make any promises until then.'

63 'Is there anybody else who could do it?'

64 'I won't be able to do this if I do that.'

65 'I'll get to it x hours/days/weeks from now.'

66 'Sorry, I'm just too busy – so-and-so might be able to do it.'

67 'Do we really need to do this now?'

68 'I'm currently full-time on such-and-such. What's the priority of this in comparison? I can do one or the other.'

Saying 'no' and your system

The previous chapter described your system and, in particular, the list. The list is where all the things contending to be done get stored. Learning to say 'no' means that you now have a way of (a) discriminating between what should get done and what shouldn't; (b) doing the things that should be done; and (c) not doing the things that shouldn't be done.

Your mission for Day 3

It's not a question of having lots of ways to say 'no'. Most anyone could come up with lists like these if they put their minds to it. The thing is to *actually* say 'no'. This, then, is your mission for Day 3.

> It's not a question of having lots of ways to say 'no'.

> The thing is to *actually* say 'no'.

Your mission for Day 3 is to say 'no' to everything or to say 'no' 20 times in succession, whichever is the longer period of time. Don't take on any new things whatsoever. Use the list above to reactively deal with any requests. But also proactively use your anti-job description to not do/decline to do things. Try and get through the whole day with a clean sheet or try to build up an uninterrupted run of twenty things that you said 'no' to. If you fail or it all goes horribly wrong, try again tomorrow until you get a whole day without accepting anything and/or an uninterrupted run of 20 'no's'.

> Routinely question everything that's given to you and to try to negotiate it rather than agree it straight up.

What you're trying to do is get to a point where it's your instinctive reaction to say 'no' rather than 'yes'. In other words, to routinely question everything that's given to you and to try to negotiate it rather than agree it straight up.

What's going to work best for you?

You'll remember the analysis you did in Chapter 1 where you looked at what stopped you from getting more done. The qustionnaire is reproduced here. This time there's an additional column. The column shows where saying 'no' would be particularly effective. If you scored high on any of the line items with an entry in the right-hand column, then saying 'no' will work well for you.

I'm stopped from getting more done because:	1 = Strongly disagree	2 = Disagree	3 = Feel neutral	4 = Agree	5 = Strongly agree	Saying 'no' particularly effective
1. Of inadequate staffing levels/staffing shortages/staff not being replaced/being under-resourced						Absolutely – the cure for inadequate staffing levels is not working more. It's matching the amount of work to be done to the amount of people to do it
2. Of having an inexperienced team/staff not trained to required level						

3. I do specialised work which cannot be easily shared					
4. Several of my projects have the same priority level					
5. Of my organisation's inability to say 'no'					That doesn't also have to be your inability
6. Of my inability to say 'no'. I'm the proverbial nice guy/gal and want to help people as much as possible					You can say 'no' and still be viewed as a nice guy/gal. Look again at the lists above
7. Of taking on too much work/too many projects					Obviously
8. Of misusing of time – not documenting and setting goals with time limits					

9. I'm not really disciplined in the management of my time					
10. I get more work and projects but don't get more resources					Don't take the work unless you get the resources
11. Of aggressive timescales within the organisation					
12. I jump from one thing to another without completing the first task					Well, don't do that then. Pick a task, do it, finish it and don't take interruptions while you're doing it. It'll make a *huge* difference.
13. I don't manage projects properly					
14. I accept more work/projects to try to gain more knowledge					That's OK, but you also need the right resources to get the job done

15. Of the pace the organisa-tion works at					
16. I have more work to do than time available to do it					
17. Of teething problems due to something being new, e.g. a new job or department or structure					
18. I over commit to other people					
19. I over commit when I take on new tasks/ projects					
20. I take on new tasks/projects before completing old ones					

21. Of a lack of knowledge of the organisation in which I work					
22. Of difficulties with estimating the work required accurately					
23. Of projects that are regarded as completed by management but still require work					
24. Of not delegating					
25. Of being too ambitious in terms of what I thought I could achieve					
26. Of the culture of the organisation					

27. Of the national culture where I work					
28. Of covering for other people on annual or sick leave					Don't be so obliging. Same comments as earlier. By all means accept these things, but you're going to need the resources as well
29. Of something not being done properly or completely so that it has to be done again					
30. Of too many people asking me to do too many things					You know what to do! Say no
31. Of people not knowing what I'm currently doing so they assume I'm not busy					Show them your dance card
32. Of multiple things to do					Obviously

33. Of moving between jobs and currently having an overlap					
34. Of accepting stuff that is not my job					Now, that's not a good idea, is it?
35. Of having too many roles					
36. That's just the way I am					So why did you buy the book? You were once a baby in nappies – but you didn't stay that way!
37. I haven't told my boss					So tell him. Show him your dance card
38. I say 'yes' to everything					So learn to say no

39. Of not asking for help					
40. I have a lot of stuff to do					
41. Of not enough time to complete all tasks to a satisfactory level					
42. Of firefighting					
43. Of bad planning					
44. Of wrong estimates					

45. People keep interrupting me so I can't follow my intended plan					
46. People don't do what they learned in training					So why not remind them of that fact when they come bothering you. Say no and they'll soon get the message
47. Of getting small things out of the way so that I can then focus on the bigger ones					
48. Of losing people to other projects					
49. I'm just not very well organised					That doesn't mean you can't learn the skills of being organised. One of these skills is saying no
50. I deal with emergencies rather than planning					

51. I don't do the most important thing first					
52. I don't like to say 'no'					Read the next section on guilt and approval seeking
53. I don't feel I can say 'no'					Sure you can. You just need a bit of practice. It's a skill – like surfing or tightrope walking
54. Projects never end completely					
55. I always prioritise other people's stuff over my own activities					
56. Of not using my time-management system					

57. Of requests coming from upper management					
58. People don't check on my availability					Why should they? It's not their job to check it. It's your job to know it and to tell them
59. Not enough time is given to planning					
60. I haven't implemented time-management training with sufficient discipline. I implemented it but then went back to my old ways					
61. I have not always prioritised the most important jobs					
62. Of constant change/ demands on my time					

63. Of not always appreciating the scale of what I've been asked to do. By the time I do, commitments have already been made and have to be delivered on					
64. People are not always available to help					
65. Of the nature of the business – things constantly change and I have to adapt					
66. There is no one else to do it					Not your problem. The management will be more than happy to let you take stuff without the necessary resources. They're not going to change, so that means you're going to have to
67. Management don't account for my current workload before giving me more work					Why should they? It's not their job to check it. It's your job to know it and to tell them

What happens if you keep on saying 'yes'?

Well, the simple answer is that they just keep giving you more. You become more stressed. Your workload does nothing but increase. You begin to drop the ball. Deadlines slip and are missed. The people for whom you work become unhappy; they start to question whether you can really do your job properly. And all of this while you're working your butt off. Could anything be more unattractive?

So if you've been saying to yourself, 'I'm not going to be able to say no' or 'I can't say no', it doesn't seem to me like you have a viable alternative.

'But I'll feel guilty', I hear you say. 'They won't like me. They'll say that I'm inflexible, that I'm not a team player.'

Read on.

Dealing with guilt

Guilt occurs when we feel we have violated some code to which we prescribe. For example, everybody in the organisation works long hours, we feel guilty because we go home early or on time! Guilt is a pretty pointless emotion – and if you're in any doubt about this, get your hands on *Your Erroneous Zones* by Wayne Dyer.[2]

You can deal with guilt by stopping the source of it and by building up your resistance to it. Here are some ways of doing that. For a fuller discussion of this topic, you can refer to Dyer's book.

Stop the sources

1   You can identify the sources of guilt by keeping a 'Guilt Journal'. Write down any things you did that made you feel guilty. What happened, when and with whom? If you keep it religiously for say, a month, it will give you some useful insights into where your guilt zones are.

2   Tackle the guilt figures head on. If people who make you feel
    guilty – people like bosses, peers, subordinates, customers –
    make any reference to your leaving on time, no matter how
    oblique, indirect or implied, give them the it's-all-about-
    achievement-not-attendance speech. You don't have to be
    obnoxious or aggressive. Merely explain how you've done what
    needs to be done and now you're heading home to the other
    part of your life. The important thing is to make sure that you
    never let one of these references go. Always catch them up –
    they'll soon stop doing it. They may even ask you what the
    secret of your success is.

3   Reconsider your value system. Which values to you really
    believe in and which do you only pretend to accept? Make two
    lists – the ones you really believe in and the ones you pay lip
    service to. Be brutal in your choices.

Build up your resistance

1   Do something which you know is bound to result in feelings of
    guilt. (This is the notion that the only way to deal with
    something you fear is to do it – see Jeffreys (1991).[3]) Leave the
    office on time. Just get up and walk out the door. Make no
    excuses, don't make up any stories, never mind who sees you,
    just get up and go. Start small. Do it once in a month. Then
    increase it to once in a week. Then twice a week. Then every
    second day. Then every day. Reward yourself as you go. Look at
    how your guilt reduces the more often you do this.

2   See whether going home on time makes you happy. Yes,
    subscribing to some sort of unfathomable code can have a
    certain satisfaction. But ask yourself whether you'd rather be
    subscribing to a code or doing your job properly and then
    enjoying life outside work. Answer honestly.

Dealing with approval-seeking

Yes, sure we all want to be loved. But nothing we do – from the opinions we hold to the actions we take to the clothes we wear to the little foibles we have – is going to please everybody. People are going to be unhappy with stuff and the sooner we get used to that notion the better.

So what can you do to reduce your need for approval and engaging in approval-seeking behaviour? Again, similar to the last section, you can stop the sources and increase your resistance.

Stop the sources

1   Realise that if someone disapproves of you, the problem is theirs and not yours. Say somebody makes a snide remark about you 'slipping out early'. In the past you might have tended to be combative – 'What's it to you? I had all my work done.' Or defensive – 'I had to go and pick up my kids' (which might or might not have been true). Or passive aggressive – gritting your teeth and saying to yourself, 'I'll get him.' Now instead, you say, 'You had to stay late, did you?' The trick is to turn the comment back on them. Beginning sentences with 'you' instead of 'I' is a masterful way of doing that.

> The trick is to turn the comment back on them. Beginning sentences with 'you' instead of 'I' is a masterful way of doing that.

2   Refuse to engage with the people who are sending you the disapproval.

Increase your resistance

1   Take the criticism head-on. This involves you naming the issue that the other person has placed between you. So you would say something like, 'Ah, you've noticed I'm trying to get out on time. Yeah, I've done a whole bunch of things to try to help me do that. If you like I can share some of them with you.'

2   Thank them for their observation. Your boss says, 'I see you're not staying back as late as you used to.' You say, 'Yes, you're right. I've been putting a lot of effort into trying to be as efficient as possible.' It defuses the whole thing.

3   On the basis that the only way to conquer a fear is to do the thing you're afraid of[4], actively invite disapproval. Deliberately do something which you know will result in disapproval. Then try to stop yourself from getting upset. By courting disapproval you'll increase your skill at dealing with it.

4   Try ignoring disapproval. Just pretend it's not there. Don't use this technique all the time, but rather mix its use in with the use of the other techniques on our list here.

5   Break the connection between other peoples' disapproval and your self-esteem. Look at your own track record of achievement. Now disconnect that from the disapproval – the disapproval is their stuff, the achievement is yours.

> Deliberately do something which you know will result in disapproval. Then try to stop yourself from getting upset. By courting disapproval you'll increase your skill at dealing with it.

CHAPTER 7

Let stuff 'go hang'

I was surprised to learn that the *Encyclopaedia Britannica* actually has a definition of 'go hang'. It says that it's 'to cease to be of interest or concern'. Having stuff ceasing to be of interest or concern is going to be very important for you going forward.

There's all this stuff contending to get done. Picture that great big mountain of stuff – that mountain that you're never going to be able to scale. And each of those bits of stuff there is saying, 'Take me!', 'Take me!', 'Take me!' But, as we've seen, lots of this stuff is going to have to go hang, if you are to achieve your goal of getting more done. Here's a whole bunch of ways of letting stuff go hang. Don't worry if there's a little bit of overlap with Chapter 6. All you need is one or two of these little fellas and they could make a big difference.

1 Ignore it (and it may just go away).

2 Ask why it has to be done and try to make the case that it's not necessary.

3 Test whether anybody uses the result of the particular activity. Say, for example, there's this report you produce regularly and it soaks up a bunch of your time. The classic way to see if it is read is to put a sentence like, 'I'll give you £10 if you read this sentence' into the report somewhere. If nobody comes to claim the £10, then it means that the thing isn't actually being read and so there's little point in you doing it. You should let it go hang.

4 Get somebody else to do it. (Delegate it is the fancier term for this.)

5 Pay somebody else to do it. That troubling piece of DIY or bit of weeding that you've been shying away from. Maybe for a little bit of money you can get the thing to go hang.

6 Don't do something.

7 Stop doing something.

8 Do 6 or 7, plus announce the fact that it's not going to be done any more.

9 Delay, stall, stonewall until eventually they stop asking for it. If that happens, then they obviously didn't want/need it enough.

10 Delete the contents of your inbox. If it's important enough it'll come back – and you can always claim the server was down and you never got it. (I suggested this at a conference I was speaking at recently. There were about 300 people in the room. There was an audible gasp when I said it!)

11 Have a 'threshold'. Above it, things are important; below it, they don't count. I mean, is it really important that the house be scrupulously tidy every day, or that the kids be bathed every night? Will it actually be that fatal if some things aren't done? (I'm not advocating slovenly living or mistreating our children or living in an unhealthy environment, but some things are really not actually that important.)

> If it never moves off the list or just keeps getting put onto the next list, then maybe it's not that important.

12 Write it on a list. If it never moves off the list or just keeps getting put onto the next list, then maybe it's not that important.

13 Save up all the 'go hang' things. Then maybe bite the bullet; set aside some time and get them done. It's not as effective as just letting them go hang completely but stalling/delaying them can buy you the time you need to get more important things done.

14 Don't answer phones – let them go to message. Don't check e-mails all the time – do it at set times every day.

15 Ask yourself 'how important is this *really*?'

Only do the right stuff

Y ou'll find that being able to say 'no' will give you a lot more time to play with, but you do need to watch carefully how you use it and ensure you only say 'yes' to the things that really matter. It's all about prioritising, so we're going to have a whole day on this key skill.

CHAPTER 8

Only do the
right stuff

Of course, you can't say 'no' to everything. There are things you have to do – for legal, contractual, moral, emotional well-being, out-of-love-for-other-people, out-of-love-for-yourself reasons. There are things you hate to do but they must be done anyway. There are things you love to do and would like to do more of. There are things you need to do because they are what you feel you are in the world for.

When you accumulate all these things, most people have a mound of stuff which, if they had 10 lifetimes, they wouldn't be able to clear.

You have one lifetime – no more than that. In that time you must sift through this great mound of stuff and identify the things that you are going to do. How you go about doing that is the subject of this chapter. Like much of the material in this book, the technique is simple. If you apply it as described, you will find yourself:

> You have one lifetime – no more than that. In that time you must sift through this great mound of stuff and identify the things that you are going to do.

● getting more done than previously;

● experiencing a far greater sense of achievement;

● with free time opening up during your day.

I then extend the basic technique to a technique known as 'vicious prioritisation'. If you can apply this successfully, then you will:

- be delighted and astonished at how much you get done and how much time becomes available to you;
- have a complete sense of control over where your time goes.

Prioritisation

Sometimes you may hear people say, 'I have 5 priority-one things to do, 13 priority-two things and 411 priority-three things.'

That's not prioritisation.

> Prioritisation is looking at the list of things you have to do and asking yourself this question: 'If I could only do one thing on this list what would it be?'

Prioritisation is looking at the list of things you have to do – you created this in Chapter 5 – and asking yourself this question: 'If I could only do one thing on this list what would it be?'

This is your number 1 priority. Then you take the remaining list and ask yourself the same question – 'If I could only do one thing on this list what would it be?' This is your number 2 priority. You continue to do this, numbering each item and then removing it from the list of things to be done, until all of the items are numbered. This numbered – prioritised – list is your priority list.

Priorities aren't absolute

Priorities can change over time. What was important today can be unimportant tomorrow. I did some work with a harassed mother and career woman who, when she did her priorities, found that her children didn't figure in the top five. Was she a bad mother? Not at all. It was just that at that point in her life, there were other things she needed to get sorted first and so, for a while, her children were going to have to wait. She planned to talk to her partner about this to see what they could come up with.

Priorities determine goals

Yes, priorities can change over time, but be careful of them changing constantly. If this happens, if your priorities are changing every day or every couple of hours, then what's more likely is that you're just firefighting – jumping from one crisis to the next. There's a benefit to thinking long and hard about your priorities because they can end up pointing you at what you really want to get out of life.

Not only that, but once you know your priorities, you can then be really ruthless about where you spend your time.

> Once you know your priorities, you can then be really ruthless about where you spend your time.

I call this 'vicious prioritisation' and talk about it more below.

Your first job on today, Day 4, is to take your list (which you created in Chapter 5) and prioritise the items on it as described above.

Now here's the next thing for you to do. It concerns objectives in your job.

Objectives in work

Everybody has objectives in work. In addition most jobs have employee appraisal systems of one sort or another. They seem to have become increasingly sophisticated and complex over the years. Balanced Score Cards, 360 degree appraisal systems, Management by Objectives, Key Result Areas, you name it.

Now what I find surprising about all this is the following. Most people I know who are subject to such systems don't know, when they are about to go in to their six-month or annual appraisal, how they are going to be rated. In fact, 'surprising' is a bit of an understatement. I find this truly incredible.

Maybe it's because I earn my living doing what are, in general, very short assignments. A three-day training course here, one day's consulting there. Given that I earn my living in this way, it's absolutely essential that I know – and my clients know – what they can expect from the period of time we're going to spend together. And it's not just that, we both need to establish – and establish very, very quickly – how I could do the best possible job and how they're going to assess me. Or to put it another way, how we will both know that I've done the best possible job. This is the first thing I do on every assignment I undertake.

You need to do the same with your boss. You need to have the conversation with him/her which begins, 'Boss, how would we both know – at the end of three months/six months/a year/whatever – that I had done the best possible job?' This could be a difficult conversation because in general, everybody is happy to settle for things like, 'Keep the customers happy' or 'Make the world a better place for bunny rabbits.'

You need to get past that kind of stuff and get down to the real, definite, measurable things. If you do, I guarantee that both you and your boss will find that your contribution to the organisation increases dramatically. You'll also find that there's a fair chance your working hours will go down.

Vicious prioritisation

Life is a problem in supply and demand. There is demand – the stuff to be done – and there is supply – the amount of time you have available to do the stuff. Given that you never have enough supply to match the demand, you need to establish where your priorities lie. One thing you can then do is to devote more time to the things that are high priority and less time to the things that aren't.

Vicious prioritisation takes this a stage further. Perfect vicious prioritisation is where you devote time to the things that are important and no time to the things that aren't. Let me give you an example.

Perfect vicious prioritisation is where you devote time to the things that are important and no time to the things that aren't.

 example

In 1999 and 2000, my company ETP, was much bigger than it is now. When the downturn in the technology sector came, we tried to ride it out. We didn't have a wholesale down-sizing. Rather, my fellow shareholders and I said that we would forego profits to keep people in jobs. Hopefully, people would see the slowdown and leave of their own accord but we wouldn't push them. Viewed purely from a business point of view, this was probably a dumb move. Maybe, karma-wise, it was good. Maybe the good karma that it sent out will come back to us. Maybe it already has.

The result of all this, however, was that we ended up with a very large – and I mean very large – debt that had to be cleared. We've cleared the bulk of it and we cleared it in a falling market, since it's only recently that the technology sector has started to turn around. During that time I had only two priorities. (In fact, these remain my two priorities. This has worked so well for me that I'm continuing to do it, even though the debt heat is pretty much gone.) They were:

1   existing customers

2   new customers.

After that anything else could go hang. I agreed this with the employees and this is what I have done ever since.

You may argue that it's a small company, it's my company, I can do anything I want. There is certainly some truth in that argument. But, assuming you work for somebody else, what happens if you don't do the right things? Your boss gets grumpy, you get a bad appraisal, your career prospects stall, worst case you get fired. But if I don't do the right things I don't eat! The stakes are actually much higher for me. So if vicious prioritisation can work for me, it can work for anybody.

The other stakeholders

If you're going to do vicious prioritisation it's important to remember that there are other people – who could be called 'stakeholders' – who have a stake in what you're going to do. In my case, it was primarily my employees. (In some ways I think of them as my bosses!) The same will be true of you. There will be other people who will be affected either positively or negatively by what you propose to do. Make a list of who they are and write down what you have to do, if anything, to get their buy-in.

In my case there were really three stakeholders – the employees, the customers (existing or future) and my dependants. With the employees, I told them that I thought I should focus on these two things in order to save the company. I asked whether that was OK with them? They agreed! The customers were probably going to fare slightly better, or at least no worse from this new arrangement so there was really no buy-in there. And my dependants? Well, from their point of view, there wasn't really a plan B, so they had to buy-in whether they liked it or not.

Where your time goes needs to reflect your priorities

I have a (female) friend who runs a family (a husband and two boys) and holds down a high-pressure, very responsible job. I asked her one day whether she found the potential conflict between the two roles very stressful.

> 'Not very often,' she replied. 'I made a decision when I took this job that the family would always come first. That makes it very easy.'
>
> 'So you don't feel guilty very often?', I asked.
>
> She smiled and said, 'I don't do guilt *at all*.'

At the risk of stating the obvious, if you're saying that certain things are important and certain things aren't, then you need to spend the bulk of your time on the things that are. Thus, measuring where your time actually goes can be something of an eye-opener. You may remember, back in Chapter 5, I said that your system needed to consist of four things. They were:

- the list;
- a way of tracking appointments;
- a filing system;
- a way of recording where your time goes.

By recording where your time goes, you can see if that reflects your priorities. If not, you can do something about it. Here's an example.

---

example

I talked at the opening of this chapter about the different types of stuff we all have in our lives. They were:

- things you have to do – for legal, contractual, moral, emotional well-being, out-of-love-for-other-people, out-of-love-for-yourself reasons;
- things you hate to do but they must be done anyway;
- things you love to do and would like to do more of;
- things you need to do because they are what you feel you are in the world for.

I've told you already that I have only two priorities but, in fact, I have three. The first two are as I said:

1 existing customers

2 new customers.

But I also have a third priority. It falls into one or both of the categories: 'things you love to do and would like to do more of', and 'things you need to do because they are what you feel you are in the world for'. I like to write books – both fiction and non-fiction. In fact, in a perfect world, I would be a fiction writer. So my three priorities are:

1 existing customers

2 new customers

3 writing.

At the moment, writing isn't enough to pay all the bills. I'd like to think that some day it will be. However, in the meantime it must take third place to the things that bring home the bacon. This is not say that sometimes I don't temporarily move it up the priority list in order, say, to get a book written. This is what I am doing as I write this with this book.

With my first and second priorities, the existing and new customers, I have to divide my time between selling and delivery. Delivery is what actually brings in the money. Not enough of that and we don't eat. But selling is what ensures that there's an ongoing stream of delivery. Not enough of that and the stream dries up. It's a delicate balancing act.

		Sales	Writing	Delivery
2006	May	3%	32%	65%
	Jun	7%	25%	69%
	Jul	11%	22%	66%
	Aug	24%	21%	55%
	Oct	25%	19%	56%
	Dec	28%	19%	53%
2007	Jan	32%	9%	59%
	Feb	36%	7%	57%
	Mar	53%	4%	43%
	Apr	47%	3%	50%
	May	43%	2%	54%
	Jun			
	Jul			
	Aug			
	Sep			
	Oct			
	Nov			
	Dec			

Last May, this is how I was spending my time. I had put a temporary push on to get a book finished. The amount of time going into delivery was too high and that going into sales was miniscule. You can see that in the intervening 12 months, I have changed things.

The next challenge is to try to bring delivery down and increase writing. Sales I'd like to leave where it is. If I can bring delivery down, I will spend less time on the road. Increasing writing will mean that I am spending a reasonably substantial amount of time on the thing I like to do most. Where my time goes will be matched to my priorities, which is exactly what I need, what all of us need.

Prioritising, vicious prioritising and your system

Now your list is prioritised and you have the skill of saying 'no'. Together these mean that you will only say 'yes' to the things that are really important to you. The more you practise vicious prioritisation, i.e. only doing work for which there is time available, the better off you will be.

What's going to work best for you?

You'll remember the analysis you did in Chapter 1 where you looked at what stopped you from getting more done. The questionnaire is reproduced here. This time I've added an additional column. The column shows where prioritising or prioritising viciously would be particularly effective. If you scored high on any of the line items with an entry in the right-hand column, then prioritising will work well for you.

I'm overloaded because:	1 = Strongly disagree	2 = Disagree	3 = Feel neutral	4 = Agree	5 = Strongly agree	Prioritising viciously parti-cularly effective
1. Of inadequate staffing levels/staffing shortages/ staff not being replaced/ being under-resourced						Absolutely – the cure for inadequate staffing levels is not working more. It's matching the amount of work to be done to the amount of people to do it
2. Of having an inexperienced team/staff not trained to the required level						Prioritise training of the team over doing the work yourself. You may take some hits in the short run. In the long run you will benefit
3. I do specialised work which cannot be easily shared						
4. Several of my projects have the same priority level						Nonsense! Talk to whoever's involved and do the if-I-could-only-do-one-thing-test with them

5. Of my organisation's inability to say 'no'					That doesn't also have to be your inability
6. Of my inability to say 'no'. I'm the proverbial nice guy/gal and want to help people as much as possible					You can say 'no' and still be viewed as a nice guy/gal. Look again at our list above
7. Of taking on too much work/too many projects					Obviously
8. Of misusing of time – not documenting and setting goals with time limits					
9. I'm not really disciplined in the management of my time					
10. I get more work and projects but don't get more resources					Don't take the work unless you get the resources

11. Of aggressive timescales within the organisation					
12. I jump from one thing to another without completing the first task					Well, don't do that then. Pick a task, do it, finish it and don't take interruptions while you're doing it. It'll make a *huge* difference
13. I don't manage projects properly					
14. I accept more work/projects to try to gain more knowledge					That's OK, but you also need the right resources to get the job done
15. Of the pace the organisation works at					
16. I have more work to do than time available to do it					Then you're going to have to prioritise because you can't carry on in this situation

17. Of teething problems due to something being new, e.g. a new job or department or structure						
18. I over commit to other people						
19. I over commit when I take on new tasks/projects						
20. I take on new tasks/projects before completing old ones						Prioritising will sort this out
21. Of a lack of knowledge of the organisation in which I work						Then you need to prioritise the building of that knowledge
22. Of difficulties with estimating the work required accurately						

23. Of projects that are regarded as completed by management but still require work					
24. Of not delegating					This again is a prioritisation problem. Identify those things that you can delegate and unload them
25. Of being too ambitious in terms of what I thought I could achieve					
26. Of the culture of the organisation					The culture of the organisation is the culture of the people in it. What you want to know is how can you make the biggest possible contribution. Work that out with your boss and prioritise based on that
27. Of the national culture where I work					See previous answer
28. Of covering for other people on annual or sick leave					Don't be so obliging. Same comments as earlier. By all means accept these things, but you're going to need the resources as well

29. Of something not being done properly or completely so that it has to be done again					
30 Of too many people asking me to do too many things					You know what to do! Say no
31. Of people not knowing what I'm currently doing so they assume I'm not busy					Show them your dance card
32. Of multiple things to do					Obviously
33. Of moving between jobs and currently having an overlap					Prioritisation would certainly help here. Maybe there are things in your old job that don't need to be done or can be done by your successor. Be sure to prioritise your new job so that you understand what's important and what's not
34. Of accepting stuff that is not my job					Now, that's not a good idea, is it?

35. Of having too many roles					Prioritise − again, in agreement with your boss or bosses. If you have multiple bosses, let *them* slug it out to decide the priority
36. That's just the way I am					So why did you buy the book? You were once a baby in nappies − but you didn't stay that way!
37. I haven't told my boss					So tell him. Show him your dance card
38. I say 'yes' to everything					So learn to say no
39. Of not asking for help					
40. I have a lot of stuff to do					Prioritise. Some of that stuff is more important than other bits

41. Of not enough time to complete all tasks to a satisfactory level					
42. Of firefighting					
43. Of bad planning					
44. Of wrong estimates					
45. People keep interrupting me so I can't follow my intended plan					
46. People don't do what they learned in training					So why not remind them of that fact when they come bothering you. Say no and they'll soon get the message

47. Of getting small things out of the way so that I can then focus on the bigger ones					It's prioritisation sure, but not a very sensible form of it!
48. Of losing people to other projects					
49. I'm just not very well organised					That doesn't mean you can't learn the skills of being organised. One of these skills is saying no
50. I deal with emergencies rather than planning					
51. I don't do the most important thing first					But if prioritised then you would!
52. I don't like to say 'no'					Read the section on guilt and approval-seeking

53. I don't feel I can say 'no'					Sure you can. You just need a bit of practice. It's a skill – like surfing or playing the piano
54. Projects never end completely					
55. I always prioritise other peoples' stuff over my own activities					Begs the question, 'why?'
56. Of not using my time-management system					
57. Of requests coming from upper management					Prioritise Prioritise Prioritise
58. People don't check on my availability					Why should they? It's not their job to check it. It's your job to know it and to tell them

59. Not enough time is given to planning					
60. I haven't implemented time-manage-ment training with sufficient discipline. I implemented it but then went back to my old ways					
61. I have not always priori-tised the most important jobs					But now you will!
62. Of constant change/ demands on my time					Prioritising would solve an awful lot of these problems
63. Of not always appreciating the scale of what I've been asked to do. By the time I do, commitments have already been made and have to be delivered on					
64. People are not always available to help					

65. Of the nature of the business – things constantly change and I have to adapt					Priorities don't change that much. The fact that things are changing so much means that the priorities haven't been set properly in the first place
66. There is no one else to do it					Not your problem. The management will be more than happy to let you take stuff without the necessary resources. They're not going to change, so that means you're going to have to
67. Management don't account for my current workload before giving me more work					Why should they? It's not their job to check it. It's your job to know it and to tell them

Do as little as
possible when
doing the
right stuff

A little planning really does go a long way to helping you achieve more, so I can't stress the importance of proper planning. Now you have a system in place; you know how to say 'no' and to focus on what matters; you are now ready to really get stuck into organising your life the way you want it to be.

CHAPTER 9

A little planning is better than a lot of firefighting

Have you ever had the following experience? Somebody comes in to you and says, 'Could you do this little thing for me? Shouldn't take you more than an hour.' Weeks or months later you're still hammering away on something that would make the labours of Hercules appear like a walk in the park.

Much of the reason why people get so little done – whether in work or outside – is that they are constantly firefighting and dealing with surprises. Yet, much of this firefighting could be avoided with some forward planning. This chapter shows how the time invested in doing a little planning will be repaid many times over as things run smoothly. The chapter shows how to do this forward planning.

Project planning

What we're really talking about here is project planning. This chapter is not intended to be an exhaustive description of project planning. If you want that then you could look, for example, at my book *Fast Projects*.[5] However, what follows can be thought of as a crash course in project planning. I'll talk about work-type situations first. Then I'll show how the same ideas can be applied to non-work situations.

What happens if you firefight instead of plan?

It's Wednesday afternoon. Your boss comes scampering in to you and says, 'We need to run a job advertisement to get a certain kind of person. Can you get it into the paper by next Friday [i.e. a week and two days from today]?'

Sounds reasonable. The paper probably has a submission deadline on Wednesday of next week. 'Sure, just tell me what you need,' you say, thereby making a commitment to your boss. Here's what happens next.

Wednesday afternoon

Your boss explains what's required. You put whatever you were doing on hold (making a mental note that you're going to have to bring it home with you to finish it because it's due tomorrow) and you draw up a proper job profile. Your boss has gone home or is at a meeting by the time you're finished so it's –

Thursday morning

Before he sees it. He's happy so now you have to find out about salary and other terms and conditions. Your boss isn't sure. Go check it with HR but be sure to come back to him for the final say-so. It takes the rest of the day to get the info from HR and on –

Friday morning

Your boss approves the job profile and the salary scales, etc. Now you draft the ad. It's Friday afternoon by now and the people you need to see the ad and sign it off – your boss, HR – have gone missing. That will have to wait until –

Monday

You still have heaps of time before the submission deadline so it's –

Tuesday

When you get your boss's sign-off. You're leaving HR with the second sign-off when the HR person says, 'You got Marketing & Sales' approval, right?'

'Marketing and Sales?', you ask. 'What do they have to do with it?'

'Since existing and new customers may see the ad, Marketing and Sales always insist that they get a final look over it – in case they can slip in any marketing and sales messages. Two ads for the price of one kind-of-thing. I think it's a good idea myself. They always come up with small changes and nearly all of them improve the final ads.'

You sigh and go off to find the person responsible for Marketing and Sales. They're on a trip, so you send them an e-mail. Despite several further e-mails and a phone call, it's actually the following –

Monday

When they get back to you. (You promised the ad for *last* Friday.) They make some small changes. You e-mail the ad to your boss and HR saying you're assuming that they've no problem with the small changes and if they have, they need to get back to you ASAP because the submission deadline is Wednesday. Silence will indicate approval. (You're half-hoping that your boss won't notice that you're running late, but he does.) His reply begins, 'Have I missed something here – I thought we were running this *last* Friday ...' You have to go over to your boss and spend time explaining what went wrong. He's not a happy bunny.

Tuesday

You call up the newspaper and tell them you want to run the ad. 'Sure, send it over', they say, 'Just make sure it's in the yah format.' Your computer won't seem to do the yah format. IT eventually sort it out for you but by then it's –

Wednesday

And you've missed the submission deadline and, despite all your pleading with the paper, they won't give you a reprieve. The ad finally runs on a Friday two weeks after you promised it to your boss.

> You carry out this method whenever any project is given to you. You don't just agree to do the project.

Now let's do it all again, but this time we'll plan our way through the same project. The method for doing this is as follows. You carry out this method whenever any project is given to you. You don't just agree to do the project. Instead you do the following.

1 Say: 'I'll take a look at it'.
2 Figure out precisely what you've been asked to do. (Notice that what you've been asked to do can change over the life of the project.)
3 Figure out the sequence of events you have to go through to get this thing done. (Add in some contingency to allow for the inevitable woopsies.)
4 Decide who's going to do what in the sequence of events.
5 Allow for the unexpected.
6 Go back to whoever asked you to do the thing and say, 'Here's what I can do.'

Planning the same project

It's Wednesday afternoon. Your boss comes scampering in to you and says, 'We need to run a job advertisement to get a certain kind of person. Can you get it into the paper by next Friday [i.e. a week and two days from today]?'

1 Say: 'I'll take a look at it'

'I dunno', you say. 'I'll take a look at it.' Then you start to work through the items mentioned above. It's still Wednesday afternoon.

2 Figure out precisely what you've been asked to do

To do this, do the following. For a lot of projects it shouldn't take more than 10 or 15 minutes (but clearly it will take a lot longer for very large undertakings).

1 Ask yourself the question, 'What event marks the end of this project?'

2 Make a list of all the project stakeholders and for each stakeholder, write down their win-conditions. A stakeholder is any individual or group of people affected either positively or negatively by your project. Win-conditions are the things that would make a successful project for that stakeholder.

3 The point in time you chose as the end point of your project should deliver all of the win-conditions. If not, the point in time needs to change or else some of the win-conditions need to change.

So, with the job advertisement project, this is what you might come up with.

1 What event marks the end of this project? It's the day when the ad runs in the paper. This point in time delivers all of the win-conditions below.

2 Make a list of all of the stakeholders and their win-conditions. Here it is.

Stakeholder	Win-conditions
Us	• Run ad that reflects well on the company and doesn't upset anybody. It also should communicate why the jobs on offer are so attractive that you'd be mad not to want to apply.
Our boss	• The ad sends out a positive message about the company

Existing employees	● Doesn't upset anybody – uses only material that is in the public domain
	● Sends out a message that the company is one that people want to work for
Potential employees	● Sends out a message that the company is one that people want to work for
Sales & Marketing	● Sends out a message that the company is expanding, and is a good company to do business with
Our customers	● Sends out a message that the company is expanding, and is a good company to do business with

Notice that what you've been asked to do can change. I mention this because it's a fact of life. Often the project you start out with is not the project you end up with. Even in the little example here to do the job advertisement, it may be, for example, that somebody hears you're running an ad and wants to take advantage of that to include a position they need to fill as well. Now further complications are introduced.

It's vital for you to realise that when a change occurs on a project there are only three ways you can deal with that change. These are:

1　You can declare it to be a significant change to the original project. The importance of this is that it's significant enough for you to go back to the stakeholders and basically say, 'All bets are off. I need to do a new plan.' This new plan can have new deadlines, new lists of jobs, a new budget – all that stuff.

2　Many of the changes that happen on projects can't be classed as significant changes. They are the day-to-day 'woopsies' that make up the project. These can be dealt with using contingency (as described below). In fact, that is why there is contingency in the plan.

3   If something isn't a significant change (or it is, but you don't have the guts to say that to the stakeholders) and if you don't have contingency in the plan (either because you didn't put it in in the first place, or else you did but then some genius took it out – and you didn't stop them), then the only other possibility is that you work more to do the extra work that this change requires.

On a healthy project all three of these options are available at any given time. On an unhealthy project only the last one is used.

3   Figure out the sequence of events you have to go through to get this thing done

1   Identify the big pieces of work to be done in the project, the bits that get you from the start to the end. (Note that there are going to have to be chunks of work that ensure that each stakeholder win-condition gets met. Win-conditions don't just get met by accident!)

2   Within each of these big pieces of work, identify the detailed jobs that have to be done.

3   Break everything down such that each job you identify is between 1 and 5 days' duration or takes 1–5 person-days of work.

4   Be as specific and concrete as possible, i.e. rather than saying 'requirements gathering' say 'Charly meets with the IT people for two days to explain his requirements.'

5   Where you don't know something, make an assumption.

6   Store all the jobs in a work breakdown structure or WBS, i.e. show the project as being made up of the big pieces of work, which in turn are made up of the smaller pieces.

The other thing you need to be aware of here is the difference between Duration and Work.

- **Duration**, sometimes also called **elapsed time**, is *how long* a particular job is going to take. It is measured in the normal units of time – hours, days, months and so on. The duration of a soccer match, for example, is 90 minutes.

- **Work**, sometimes called **effort**, is how much work in a particular job. It is measured in units like man-days, person-hours, person-years and so on. The work in a soccer match, if we count two teams of 11, a referee, 2 linesmen and a fourth official is 26 times 90 minutes, i.e. 39 person-hours.

Durations are important because they enable us to figure out *how long* all or part of a project will take. Efforts are important because they enable us to figure out *how much* all or part of a project will cost.

Here we go then for the job advertisement project.

No.	Job	Depends on	Effort (in person-hours)	Duration (in days)	Notes
1	Draft up job profile	Request from boss	2	Wednesday	
2	Draw up job ad	Job no. 1	2	Thursday	
3	Get approvals (boss, HR, any others required?)	Job no. 2	2	Friday	Find out as early as possible if HR and boss will be available on Friday. Find out as early as possible if any other approvals required. Do both of these things before Job no. 1

Notice that as you start to build the sequence of events, lots of issues crop up. These are issues which, if we hadn't done the forward planning, would have turned into firefights – at least, the vast majority of them would. By uncovering them and factoring them into our sequence of events, we can try to stop them from becoming firefights. Here's our list, revised to take account of the issues to do with approvals.

No.	Job	Depends on	Effort (in person hours)	Duration (in days)	Notes
1	Find out if boss and HR available Friday. Find out if other approvals required	Request from boss	1	Wednesday	
2	Draft up job profile	Job no. 1	2	Wednesday	
3	Draw up job ad	Job no. 2	2	Thursday	
4	Get approvals (boss, HR, any others required?)	Job no. 3	2	Friday	
5	Do minor changes			Monday	We're not assuming that the approvals will work first time. Instead we're saying that minor changes may be needed. These will be made and sent back to the relevant parties

▶

No.	Job	Depends on	Effort (in person hours)	Duration (in days)	Notes
6	Get sign-offs	Job no. 5	2	Tuesday morning	Will send out an e-mail saying that if we don't hear from you by lunchtime on Tuesday, then we assume you agree
7	Put into format for newspaper	Job no. 6	1	Tuesday afternoon	Check with IT as early as possible that this isn't going to cause a problem
8	Send to paper	Job no. 7	1	Tuesday close of business	

Two other things you can usefully check early here – one is the IT thing in job 7, the other is to find out the exact submission deadline. So now our plan looks like this:

No.	Job	Depends on	Effort (in person hours)	Duration (in days)	Notes
1	● Find out if boss and HR available Friday. ● Find out if other approvals required ● Find out from newspaper what format required and when submission deadline is	Request from boss	2	Wednesday afternoon	
2	Draft up job profile	Job no. 1	2	Wednesday afternoon	

3	Draw up job ad	Job no. 2	2	Thursday	
4	Get approvals (boss, HR, any others required?)	Job no. 3	2	Friday	
5	Do minor changes			Monday morning	We're not assuming that the approvals will work first time. Instead we're saying that minor changes may be needed. These will be made and sent back to the relevant parties
6	Get sign-offs	Job no. 5	2	Monday afternoon, Tuesday morning	Will send out an e-mail saying that if we don't hear from you by lunchtime on Tuesday, then we assume you agree
7	Put into format for newspaper	Job no. 6	1	Tuesday afternoon	Check with IT as early as possible that this isn't going to cause a problem
8	Send to paper	Job no. 7	1	Tuesday close of business	
9	Contingency	Job no. 8		Wednesday	Assuming that Wednesday, close of business, is the submission deadline, then this will give us an extra day to cover delays or things going wrong

4 Decide who's going to do what in the sequence of events

Here's the plan again, this time with an extra column for who's going to do the work.

No.	Job	Depends on	Effort (in person hours)	Duration (in days)	Notes	Who
1	• Find out if boss and HR available Friday. • Find out if other approvals required • Find out from newspaper what format required and when submission deadline is	Request from boss	2	Wednesday afternoon		You
2	Draft up job profile	Job no. 1	2	Wednesday afternoon		You. Between this and the preceding job, this is going to take up all of your Wednesday afternoon
3	Draw up job ad	Job no. 2	2	Thursday		
4	Get approvals (boss, HR, any others required?)	Job no. 3	2	Friday	Have you checked that boss and HR are around. Also need an approval	

					from Sales & Marketing. Have found somebody there to do it	
5	Do minor changes			Monday morning	We're not assuming that the approvals will work first time. Instead we're saying that minor changes may be needed. These will be made and sent back to the relevant parties	You
6	Get sign-offs	Job no. 5	2	Monday afternoon, Tuesday morning	Will send out an e-mail saying that if we don't hear from you by lunchtime on Tuesday, then we assume you agree	You; boss; HR; Sales & Marketing

No.	Job	Depends on	Effort (in person hours	Duration (in days)	Notes	Who
7	Put into format for newspaper	Job no. 6	1	Tuesday afternoon	Check with IT as early as possible that this isn't going to cause a problem	You. (IT has told you how to do it)
8	Send to paper	Job no. 7	1	Tuesday close of business		You
9	Contingency	Job no. 8		Wednesday	Assuming that Wednesday, close of business, is the submission deadline, then this will give us an extra day to cover delays or things going wrong	You – if you end up needing it

5 Allow for the unexpected

Unexpected stuff happens on projects. Most of it is *bad* stuff in that it will negatively affect the project. For this you need to put contingency in the plan to allow for these inevitable (but as yet, unknown) things.

But you can also do something a bit smarter. You can do what's known as risk analysis. In risk analysis you try to anticipate what might go wrong on the project. That by itself is a useful thing to do. But you can do better than that. Not only can you anticipate what might go wrong on the project, you can then put some things into your plan to stop them things from happening. Here's a risk analysis for the run a job advertisement project to illustrate the technique. You

> Not only can you anticipate what might go wrong on the project, you can then put some things into your plan to stop them from happening.

take the actions from the risk analysis and make them part of your plan, i.e. the jobs from the risk analysis become jobs in your sequence of events.

Risk analysis

Risk	Likelihood (L) 1 = Low 2 = Medium 3 = High	Impact (I) 1 = Low 2 = Medium 3 = High	Exposure = L x I	Actions
1. People not available to do sign-offs	3	3	9	Book them well in advance
2. Miss newspaper deadline	2	3	6	Understand well in advance exactly what it is
3. Problems with the format in which the ad must go to the newspaper	3	3	9	Sort it out with the newspaper and IT well in advance. Do a test if necessary

6 Go back to whoever asked you to do the thing and say: 'Here's what I can do.'

On the basis of this plan, you go back to your boss and say, 'Yes, I can do this thing, provided you're available to sign off things here and here.' With the work you have done here there'd be every likelihood that this project would work out.

Project management in non-work situations

A few years ago two friends of mine decided to take their children to EuroDisney. They told me their plan. Fly to Paris on Friday evening arriving late. Saturday morning, after breakfast, they would travel out from central Paris to EuroDisney, spend the day there, visit all the good rides, come back, put the children to bed with a babysitter, have a bath to wind down, dress up and go out for a great French dinner.

When I heard this I was astonished at how much they were proposing to pack into the day. When I did a little bit of project management, my suspicions were confirmed. Here was their plan, whether they knew it or not.

Depart hotel	09:00	
Paris – EuroDisney	09:00–11:00	
A day at EuroDisney	11:00–19:00	Has to be a minimum of eight hours
EuroDisney – Paris	19:00–21:00	
Kids to bed	21:00–22:00	Be doing well to get them to bed in an hour
Bath to wind down	22:00–23:00	At least an hour to get any value from it
Dress up	23:00–24:00	
Find/get to restaurant	0:00–00:30	It's now Sunday. Gonna find a restaurant in the middle of the night? In Paris, yes probably
Nice relaxing dinner	00:30–03:00	Relaxed? They'll be comatose!

I'm not suggesting that whenever you think of doing anything you always get the flipchart out in the kitchen to build the plan or type a whole bunch of stuff into a project-planning tool like Microsoft

Project. What I am saying though, is that planning can be applied to anything and that there can be a lot of value in building a little sequence of events like the one above. It often only takes a few minutes and can save disappointment, waste of time, effort and money, tears, dashed expectations, lost opportunities, arguments, conflict and general all-round angst. Which is surely a good thing.

Planning and your system

You have your prioritised list and you know how to say 'no' so that only the right things get done. When you come to do one of these things ensure you do it as effortlessly as possible by planning it before you get stuck into it.

What's going to work best for you?

You'll remember the analysis you did in Chapter 1 where I got you to look at what stopped you from getting more done. The questionnaire is reproduced here. This time I've added an additional column. The column shows where a little planning would be particularly effective. If you scored high on any of the line items with an entry in the right-hand column, then a little planning will work well for you.

I'm stopped from getting more done because:	1 = Strongly disagree	2 = Disagree	3 = Feel neutral	4 = Agree	5 = Strongly agree	Prioritising viciously particularly effective
1. Of inadequate staffing levels/staffing shortages/ staff not being replaced/ being under-resourced						Absolutely – the cure for inadequate staffing levels is not working more. It's matching the amount of work to be done to the amount of people to do it
2. Of having an inexperienced team/staff not trained to the required level						Prioritise training of the team over doing the work yourself. You may take some hits in the short run. In the long run you will benefit

3. I do specialised work which cannot be easily shared						Build a sequence of events for this work. Then start to train other people and delegate pieces of the work to them. Eventually you may be able to get it all to them
4. Several of my projects have the same priority level						Nonsense! Talk to whoever's involved and do the if-I-could-only-do-one-thing-test with them
5. Of my organisation's inability to say 'no'						That doesn't also have to be your inability
6. Of my inability to say 'no'. I'm the proverbial nice guy/gal and want to help people as much as possible						You can say 'no' and still be viewed as a nice guy/gal. Look again at our list above
7. Of taking on too much work/too many projects						Obviously
8. Of misusing of time – not documenting and setting goals with time limits						Planning would get over a lot of these problems

9. I'm not really disciplined in the management of my time					But from now on you can start to use our three big principles
10. I get more work and projects but don't get more resources					Don't take the work unless you get the resources
11. Of aggressive timescales within the organisation					A good plan will show the difference between an aggressive timescale and a situation where everybody's completely lost the plot
12. I jump from thing to another without completing the first task					Well, don't do that then. Pick it up, do it, finish it and don't take interruptions while you're doing it. It'll make a *huge* difference
13. I don't manage projects properly					Well, you'll have no reason to say that after this chapter
14. I accept more work/projects to try to gain more knowledge					That's OK, but you also need the right resources to get the job done

15. Of the pace the organisa-tion works at					The answer to this is the same as the answer to question 11 above
16. I have more work to do than time available to do it					Then you're going to have to prioritise because you can't carry on in this situation
17. Of teething problems due to something being new, e.g. a new job or department or structure					A good plan would have anticipated a lot of these. You could have assumed some level of teething problems and factored time into the plan accordingly
18. I over commit to other people					A good plan will stop you from doing this
19. I over commit when I take on new tasks/projects					A good plan will also stop you from doing this
20. I take on new tasks/projects before completing old ones					Prioritising will sort this out

21. Of a lack of knowledge of the organisation in which I work					Then you need to prioritise the building of that knowledge
22. Of difficulties with estimating the work required accurately					Good plans = good estimates. We showed you above how to build accurate estimates
23. Of projects that are regarded as completed by management but still require work					If you had planned the thing properly and, in particular, identified, what was going to mark the end of the project, this wouldn't have happened
24. Of not delegating					This again is a prioritisation problem. Identify those things that you can delegate and unload them
25. Of being too ambitious in terms of what I thought I could achieve					A good plan will tell you what's possible and what's not
26. Of the culture of the organisation					The culture of the organisation is the culture of the people in it. What you want to know is how you can make the biggest possible contribution. Work that out with your boss and prioritise based on that ased on that

27. Of the national culture where I work						See previous answer
28. Of covering for other people on annual or sick leave						Don't be so obliging. Same comments as earlier. By all means accept these things, but you're going to need the resources as well
29. Of something not being done properly or completely so that it has to be done again						Plan it, estimate it properly and insist on getting the time the plan says to do the job properly
30. Of too many people asking me to do too many things						You know what to do! Say no
31. Of people not knowing what I'm currently doing so they assume I'm not busy						Show them your dance card
32. Of multiple things to do						Obviously

33. Of moving between jobs and currently having an overlap					Prioritisation would certainly help here. Maybe there are things in your old job that don't need to be done or can be done by your successor. Be sure to prioritise your new job so that you understand what's important and what's not
34. Of accepting stuff that is not my job					Now, that's not a good idea, is it?
35. Of having too many roles					Prioritise – again in agreement with your boss or bosses. If you have multiple bosses, let *them* slug it out to decide the priority
36. That's just the way I am					So why did you buy the book? You were once a baby in nappies – but you didn't stay that way!
37. I haven't told my boss					So tell him. Show him your dance card
38. I say 'yes' to everything					So learn to say no

39. Of not asking for help					Your plan will show where you need help. Your plan will also show the effect of not asking for it (or not getting it)
40. I have a lot of stuff to do					Prioritise. Some of that stuff is more important than other bits
41. Of not enough time to complete all tasks to a satisfactory level					Build a realistic plan. This will show you what time is required. Then insist on the time
42. Of firefighting					All together now – 'A little planning is better than a lot of firefighting'
43. Of bad planning					So do good planning as described above
44. Of wrong estimates					So do better estimates

45. People keep interrupting me so I can't follow my intended plan					Factor the interruptions into the plan. If you know there's going to be a level of interruption as you carry out your plan, the dumbest thing you could do would be to assume there won't be any
46. People don't do what they learned in training					So why not remind them of that fact when they come bothering you. Say no and they'll soon get the message
47. Of getting small things out of the way so that I can then focus on the bigger ones					It's prioritisation sure, but not a very sensible form of it!
48. Of losing people to other projects					If you lose people to other projects, adjust your plan accordingly and show the project stakeholders what the effect of that is going to be
49. I'm just not very well organised					That doesn't mean you can't learn the skills of being organised. One of these skills is saying no

50. I deal with emergencies rather than planning						But you won't do that from now on, will you? Once again, 'a little planning is better than a lot of firefighting'
51. I don't do the most important thing first						But if prioritised, then you would!
52. I don't like to say 'no'						Read the section on guilt and approval-seeking
53. I don't feel I can say 'no'						Sure you can. You just need a bit of practice. It's a skill – like surfing or playing the piano.
54. Projects never end completely						But if they're planned properly, they will
55. I always prioritise other peoples' stuff over my own activities						Begs the question, 'why?'
56. Of not using my time-management system						Three principles – that's all you need to remember and practise

57. Of requests coming from upper management					Prioritise Prioritise Prioritise
58. People don't check on my availability					Why should they? It's not their job to check it. It's your job to know it and to tell them
59. Not enough time is given to planning					But you're going to change all that, aren't you? It's the single most important thing to do when you're given a project
60. I haven't implemented time-management training with sufficient discipline. I implemented it but then went back to my old ways					Maybe just having three principles will make it easier
61. I have not always prioritised the most important jobs					But now you will!
62. Of constant change/ demands on my time					Prioritising would solve an awful lot of these problems

63. Of not always appreciating the scale of what I've been asked to do. By the time I do, commitments have already been made and have to be delivered on						Planning will stop this problem from ever recurring
64. People are not always available to help						So, adjust the plan and show the stakeholders the implications of people not being available
65. Of the nature of the business – things constantly change and I have to adapt						Priorities don't change that much. The fact that things are changing so much means that the priorities haven't been set properly in the first place
66. There is no one else to do it						Not your problem. The management will be more than happy to let you take stuff without the necessary resources. They're not going to change, so that means you're going to have to
67. Management don't account for my current workload before giving me more work						Why should they? It's not their job to check it. It's your job to know it and to tell them

CHAPTER 10

Sequences of events and your well-being

You'll remember the method for planning in the previous chapter:

1 Say: 'I'll take a look at it.'
2 Figure out precisely what you've been asked to do. (Notice that what you've been asked to do can change over the life of the project.)
3 Figure out the sequence of events you have to go through to get this thing done. (Add in some contingency to allow for the inevitable woopsies.)
4 Decide who's going to do what in the sequence of events.
5 Allow for the unexpected.
6 Go back to whoever asked you to do the thing and say, 'Here's what I can do.'

There is another value entirely to building sequences of events as described in step 3. Have you ever been worried about a particular thing? It seemed enormous or complicated or intimidating. You didn't know where to start or you didn't want to start, the thing was so unpleasant.

You know the kind of thing. A tax return? You hate the form-filling or, worse still, you're dreading what the result will show. A piece of DIY? You're not entirely confident about your expertise and dread cocking it up completely – or, worse still, that you'll damage/destroy things that are already there. A house move? Where are you going to start? That tricky conversation with the bank manager? It's too scary. Best not to think about it, never mind pick up the phone. Except that you can't stop thinking about it. It hovers in your mind like a black cloud. It soaks up your energy. It causes you to worry or lose sleep. It dissipates your strength whenever you think about it.

Now look at how sequences of events can help you. Let's take the tax return.

Tax return example

Don't let it sit there, hoping it will go away. Instead make a sequence of events. Here's a possible one:

1 Go right through form; fill in as much as possible; make a list of supporting stuff that you need. (At the end of this job, you'll have the form partially filled in and you'll probably find that there's other stuff that you need to get to attach to the tax return. Until you've done job number 1, let's make an assumption that it's going to turn out that there are *four* such things, i.e. four supporting pieces of information/forms/documents. Obviously, you could have assumed any number. These will then become the next four (or however many it turns out to be) items in the sequence of events.)

2 Get piece of information/form/document number 1.

3 Get piece of information/form/document number 2.

4 Get piece of information/form/document number 3.

5 Get piece of information/form/document number 4.

6 Finalise form.

7 Put package (form and supporting stuff) together.

8 Send it off.

There now, it took a few minutes to put together the sequence of events but now look at the result. This little project – for such it is – has shape to it. You don't have to start on it all, just take the first step in the sequence. Do that step and decide when you're going to do the next one. Each time you get a step done, you'll get a little burst of pleasure that you're making progress. Part-way through you'll see how much progress you've made. There'll be no dark cloud of worry in your head because you'll know you're making progress and that it's in hand and under control. Finally, at the end, will come the happy day when you send it off and you're done. That particular unpleasant task is out of the way.

DIY example

1   Get the tools.

2   Get the materials.

3   Figure out the sequence of events (list of jobs) to get the task done. Often DIY manuals give you this, or you can find it on the Internet or at DIY stores.

4   For each of the jobs, do you think you could reasonably give it a shot?

5   What's the worst that could happen if you get one of these tasks wrong?

6   Are you prepared to run the risk? Do you have a backup if it does go wrong?

So here's what your sequence of events might look like:

Job	Can you give it a shot?	What's the backup?
1 Get the tools		
2 Get the materials		
3 First job in the sequence		
4 Second job in the sequence		
5 ...		
6 Final job in the sequence		

If you have all yeses in the middle column, then you're in great shape. If you have some noes, do you have a backup for those? For example, if one of the jobs is to remove, say, a radiator from a central heating system and it all goes horribly wrong, do you have the number of a plumber? More immediately, do you also have something to block the pipe and catch the water? And if you're asking yourself questions like this, maybe you should be calling a plumber in the first place. But then, if you don't take risks like this then you never learn. Ah, the rich tapestry of human life!

House-move example

Here's a possible sequence of events.

1 Go from room to room and make a list of everything that has to be moved.
2 Decide whether to do it yourself or get somebody. If you're getting somebody, are you going to box the stuff or them? (Let's assume you decide to do it yourself.)
3 Get packing cartons.
4 Arrange hire of van.
5 Go from room to room and pack stuff into cartons.
6 On the day of the move pick up van.
7 Load van.
8 Drive across town.
9 Unpack stuff.
10 Repeat steps 7–9 until done.
11 Return van.

Tricky conversation with the bank manager

1   Decide what you're trying to get from the conversation.

2   Decide what supporting info you'll need. (Try and see the conversation from the bank manager's point of view. What questions is s(he) likely to be asking? What information will s(he) need to make his/her decision?)

3   Get this info.

4   Make the call.

So, in summary, you can very much reduce the amount of worry, stress, guilt and fear that life throws at you by dealing with any undertaking in this way. It's a nice side-effect of the principle that a little planning is better than a lot of firefighting.

> A little planning is better than a lot of firefighting.

DAY 6

Some other skills

A long with the core time-blasting skills you've learnt in the past five days, you'll need just a few more things to set you well and truly on the way to getting more done. On Day 6 you'll find out how it is actually possible to plan the unplanned, how to create extra time in your life *and* I'm going to give you lots of help to avoid the dreaded s-word – STRESS.

CHAPTER 11

Planning the unplanned

t may sound a like a contradiction in terms. In fact, it's the easiest thing in the world to do. It's also another useful weapon in the war to get more done.

You may remember in Chapter 5 that I described 'the system' and I said that one of the things you needed in your system was a way of recording where your time goes. This is one of the places that you can use this. Here's what you do.

Record how much of your time per day goes into unplanned stuff. Do it over a week or a couple of weeks. Let's say it ends up looking like this after two weeks.

Day	Mon	Tue	Wed	Thu	Fri	Mon	Tue	Wed	Thu	Fri
Time spent on unplanned stuff (in hours)	2	3	2.5	6.5	3.5	4	3	3	2	0.5

This is 30 hours over 10 days, or 3 hours per day. So, based on this average, you should plan for three hours of each of your days being soaked up by unplanned work. So make this part of your daily load – which means that you only have five hours a day (not eight!) left over to do other work.

Let's say then that your next two weeks looked like this:

Day	Mon	Tue	Wed	Thu*	Fri	Mon*	Tue*	Wed*	Thu	Fri
Time spent on unplanned stuff (in hours)	1.5	2.5	3.0	7	3	3.5	3.5	3.5	1.5	3

With the three hours a day, you would only have problems on the days marked with an asterisk. Furthermore, you could now adjust your three hours upwards, since in this second fortnightly period, the time spent on unplanned stuff has gone up to 32 hours over the 10 days.

By continuously doing this you would be able to maintain a very accurate prediction of how much of your time is going to go into unplanned stuff. This will mean that to those around you – notably your boss – you'll appear cool as a cucumber, completely in control and able to deal with anything s(he) throws your way. What an asset to the organisation!

CHAPTER 12

How to create extra time in your life

'm as busy as the next person and there are some days that are complete washouts where, dawn to dusk, it's just frantic. But it's only *some* days – and to be honest, there aren't that many of them. I have lots of days where I get lots done but there's still space, extra time where I don't have to do anything in particular.

Dance cards, as described on Day 1, are one way of doing this. You put an item into your dance card called 'Time for me' or 'Time out' or something like that. You then prioritise it appropriately and provided you've got your supply and demand under control, i.e. you're practising vicious prioritisation, you should be able to get that time.

Here's another way. It enables you to try to find the time every day.

1   Absolutely first thing, or better still last thing the previous night, make a list of everything you'd like to get done on this particular day.

> Absolutely first thing, or better still last thing the previous night, make a list of everything you'd like to get done on this particular day.

2   Include on your list the 'Time for me' or 'Time out' as above.

3   This list is your list of contenders – your list of things that could be done.

4   Now mark each item on the list with one of the letters 'A', 'B', 'C', 'D'.

5   Here's what the letters mean:

- 'A'. I have to get this done today. Planets will collide, stars will fall, bosses will be grumpy, share prices will nose-dive if this thing isn't done. Notice too that it's perfectly acceptable for your 'Time for me'/'Time out' to be an 'A'. Be as vicious as you can about the 'A's. Is it really that important? Why couldn't it wait? See also number 10, below.

- 'B'. It'd be nice to get it done today.

- 'C'. Realistically, I'm not going to get this done today.

- 'D'. Delegate it. I can get somebody else to do this.

6 Do all the 'D's first, i.e. get these items delegated.

7 Now do all the 'A's.

8 When you're finished all the 'A's stop. Go home. Go on – go! Away with you! Off you go! You may have got your 'Time for me'/'Time out' during the day as a result of making it an 'A'. Alternatively, you'll almost definitely be getting out earlier than you would have otherwise.

9 A few other possibilities. What happens if something new comes in during the day? Well then, what you do is you insert this item onto your list and give it an 'A' through 'D' classification. Then you do it if it's an 'A' or a 'D'. If this results in your day being messed up, you need to read the previous chapter, Chapter 11, again and do what it says.

10 What happens if the end of the day comes and one of your 'A's isn't done? Well then, it can't have been an 'A', can it? Notice when this happens and use this knowledge to make your classification of 'A's more vicious and strict. You should soon get really good at it.

11 Finally, here's a nifty idea. If you get all of today's 'A's done, rather then going home you could start doing tomorrow's work. In other words, make tomorrow's list, classify the items 'A' through 'D', delegate the 'D's and start on the 'A's. Now you're doing tomorrow's work today! I have a friend who calls this 'working ahead'. Look at the amount of time this could give you at the end of a couple of days or a week.

CHAPTER 13

Why you'll be able to get more done

You'll remember that in Chapter 3 you analysed what things you had done in the past to try to fix your situation and why those things hadn't worked. That list is reproduced here. This time there's an additional column which shows how – using the skills you now have – you can overcome the issues which defeated you the last time.

This time there's an additional column which shows how – using the skills you now have – you can overcome the issues which defeated you the last time.

Take a look at the following questionnaire and score each of the statements on a scale of 1–5 where:

1 = Strongly disagree

2 = Disagree

3 = Feel neutral

4 = Agree

5 = Strongly agree.

I haven't been able to fix this because:	1 = Strongly disagree	2 = Disagree	3 = Feel neutral	4 = Agree	5 = Strongly agree	What things can you now do?
1. People keep interrupting me so that I can't follow my intended plan						<ul><li>Plan each day, i.e. make a list of the things that have to be done that day. Make this list the first thing you do that day or the last thing you did the previous day</li><li>Use red time and green time to structure your day, if that will help</li><li>Categorise your list using 'A' through 'D'</li><li>Do all the 'D's and 'A's</li><li>When you pick an item up to do it, don't take any interruptions until you've put it down and it's finished</li></ul>
2. People don't do what they learned in training and keep coming to me for help						<ul><li>Don't help them</li><li>Or write a FAQ (frequently asked questions) list</li><li>Or tell them politely that it's in the manual</li></ul>

3. I try to get the small things out of the way so that I can focus on the important things; but then I find that I don't have enough time for the important things					• Do the opposite. You need to make sure that the big things get done. So: • Know what those big things are – they will determine the 'A's on your daily list • When you pick an 'A' item up to do it, don't take any interruptions until you've put it down and it's finished
4. Extra resources are not available					• So match what can be done to the resources that *are* available • Use dance cards to figure out what resourcing is available, i.e. what amount of people-time is available • Use plans to figure out what resourcing is required, i.e. the amount of work (not duration) required • Then these two need to match. It's a mathematical problem and that's how you present it to your boss or other stakeholders

5. I keep losing people to other projects					● If you do, that's a significant change to your project (see Chapter 9). It certainly should not be dealt with by using contingency and absolutely not by working more
6. I feel that I just don't have any choice. This is the hand I've been dealt. I've made my bed, as the saying goes, and so I must lie in it					● This book is packed with choices – alternative things you can do to get you out of the situation you're in. If you do them they'll work. All that's required is that you do them
7. I keep dealing with emergencies ('firefighting') rather than planning					● And why on earth would you do that? Use Chapter 9 and your life will be so much easier
8. I don't know how to organise/pla n projects properly					● But if you read Chapter 9 you will

9. Work keeps coming					• Of course it does. And some of it doesn't have to be done at all. Some of it is more important than the rest of it • Identify what's important by prioritising your list and agreeing those priorities with your boss and other stakeholders • Then do these things and let everything else go hang • Make sure that when you do them you plan them properly and so that will save you lots of time
10. The more work I complete, the more work comes to me					• And why should this be a surprise? • Agree your priorities with your boss and/or other stakeholders • When more work comes to you, see whether or not it aligns with your priorities • If it does, do it • If it doesn't, let it go hang • Make sure that when you do the things you do do, you plan them properly and so that will save you lots of time

11. I don't do the most important things first					• Well silly you! Know what the most important things are (know and have agreed your priorities) • Do them • When you do them, plan them first so that you do the least amount of work possible
12. Of lack of time to try to get on top of the problem. (It's hard to drain the swamp when you're up to your neck in alligators)					• Why not do this? Record how much of your time goes into dealing with this problem, say, over a week • Now figure out (i.e. plan using Chapter 9) how much time it would take you to get the thing solved once and for all • What do the sums tell you?
13. I don't like to say 'no'					• Then you need to practise the Day 3 stuff again • Maybe also look at the bits on guilt and approval-seeking in Chapter 6 • You can also get your hands on Wayne Dyer's book[6]

14. I don't feel I can say 'no'						• You can! • So you need to practise the Day 3 stuff again • Maybe also look at the bits on guilt and approval-seeking in Chapter 6 • You can also get your hands on Wayne Dyer's book[7]
15. I just have too many things on the go						• Everybody does, for heaven's sake. This book is all about dealing with those things. You have the skills – just go and apply them
16. I always prioritise things involving other people over stuff I have to do myself						• So you won't be doing that any more, now will you? • Identify – in conjunction with your boss and other stakeholders – your own priorities • Then do those and let the rest go hang
17. I have a time-management system but I don't use it						• Really? And that's a good idea because ...?

18. Of requests that come from upper management					• Either they align with your priorities or they don't • Clarify with your boss/ other stakeholders/ upper management, if necessary whether these requests are part of your priorities or not • Then act accordingly
19. People don't check on my availability					• Why should they? Surely that's your job? • But even assuming that they should, make your dance card available to them
20. I don't devote enough time to planning					• Well aren't you a silly billy now? If you did, your life would be a whole lot easier
21. I haven't implemented my time-management training with sufficient discipline. I implemented it and then went back to my old habits					• And that was a really good idea, wasn't it?

22. I have not always prioritised the most important jobs						● But you will now, won't you?
23. Of constant change/ demands on my time						● But if you agree your priorities with your boss and other stakeholders, you won't have the problem of constant change in the demands on your time ● As for constant demands on your time, we all have those. The tools in this book are about dealing with those demands
24. I don't always appreciate the scale of what I've been asked to do. By the time I do, commitments have already been made and have to be delivered on						● Which is one of the reasons why this book has a Chapter 9
25. Of the culture of the organisation						● The culture of the organisation is the culture of the people in it. It's not just the culture of the CEO or the senior manage-ment team. If you change your behaviour, then the culture of the organisation changes

26. Of my own personality/ culture. I'm the proverbial nice guy/gal and want to help people as much as possible					• So you over-commit, you stress yourself and sometimes you fail to make these crazy targets you set yourself • Read the piece on approval-seeking in Chapter 6 • Get a hold of Wayne Dyer's book[8]. Go and buy it as a matter of urgency
27. People are not always available to help					• So build your plan around when they are available. If anyone asks why things are taking so long, say that it's because people are not always available to help. Show them the numbers in the plan – the demand (amount of work to be done) and the supply (people-time available to do the work)

| 28. Of the nature of the business – things constantly change and I have to adapt | | | | | | <ul><li>All businesses constantly change. But your priorities can change to keep up with these</li><li>Every time the business changes its priorities, go talk to your boss and change your priorities, if necessary</li><li>If these business's priorities are changing on such a rapid basis, then maybe it doesn't have priorities – and then that must be a very interesting business indeed!</li><li>And OK, you can't change how the business is run but you can ensure that your work-to-be-done (demand) matches your availability-to-do-the-work (supply). Use a dance card to show this to your boss/ stakeholders</li></ul> |

29. There is no one else to do it						• Not your problem • Use a dance card to show demand and supply • Use it to make the case to get more people • If more people can't be got, then prioritise in conjunction with your boss and other stakeholders • Then make sure that the important things get done and let the rest go hang
30. I can't change my boss						• And you've tried, have you? • And you've tried by showing him your dance card, have you? • And even if it's true, you can change yourself and your own behaviour

31. Projects are often last minute						● Yeah, so? ● Whether they're last minute or not, plan them and then tell the stakeholders what you can do
32. There are no extra resources available						● Not your problem ● Use a dance card to show demand and supply ● Use it to make the case to get more people ● If more people can't be got, then prioritise in conjunction with your boss and other stakeholders ● Then make sure that the important things get done and let the rest go hang
33. I haven't explained the problem to my boss						● So why don't you – and make sure you have the numbers (supply and demand in a dance card) available to show him/her and make your case

34. I haven't tried to address the problem					● But you will now, won't you?
35. I need to quantify the problem					● And you have all the necessary tools (a dance card) for doing that

CHAPTER 14

Don't get stressed

I t is my hope that, with the help of this book, a lot of stress will go out of your life. So far, I've been tackling this objective indirectly by trying to get you to spend more of your time in the areas that are important to you. Here I tackle it directly with some techniques that can go straight as an arrow to the stress in your life and reduce or eliminate it.

> ... some techniques that can go straight as an arrow to the stress in your life and reduce or eliminate it.

I'm pretty good with stress. Not too much causes me to worry and as a result, I've been accused of being 'cold' and 'unfeeling' because I don't worry enough. Other people clearly have a problem with my not worrying. But it is one of the things about myself that I really like. Whatever else about me, my life won't end prematurely due to stress. At least not if I have anything to do with it.

This is not to say that I don't worry at all. Potentially life and death things, such as the birth of my children, I'm not always good at. And occasionally I let worries about money mess me around for a while. But notice what I wrote there. I said '*I let* worries about money mess me around.' Yes, I let them. And just as I let them, I can *not* let them. I can make a different choice. Here are some ways of doing that.

1 **If you can do something about a particular issue, do it**. If not, say to yourself that you won't think about it again until a particular day or a particular time or until a particular event happens. Remember, too, that much of the world shuts down at the weekend.

2 If the problem seems big and unknown and scary, write down the sequence of events that will be necessary to resolve it. Now start doing the first item in the sequence. When that is done, take on the next one and then the next one and then the next one. If you come to an item where you're waiting on somebody else to do something, then apply the previous technique (number 1) until it's time for you to take up the fight again.

3 Savour the moment. You can't do anything about the past, so no point in feeling guilty about that. You can't do anything about the future, so no point in worrying about it. Just be in the moment – and, especially if things are nice just now, don't ruin them by fretting about the future or agonising over the past.

4 Do something physical – the more demanding the better.

5 Go out and enjoy nature. Go to the park or the beach or the mountains. Walk by a river or a canal or the sea. Feel the sun on your back, or rain on your face. Listen to the birds or see if you can find a place where there are no human sounds. Look at the colours. Touch things – leaves, rocks, trees. Say to yourself that it's good to be alive.

6 Keep a sense of proportion. Look at the news or read a paper if you want to get a sense of who really has problems in the world.

7 Remember that emotions don't control you. You can control them. You can *choose* to think different thoughts or feel different feelings. Mr. Dyer[9] has good stuff to say about this.

8 Try treating whatever's eating away at you as a game.

9 How will you view this particular issue a year from now? Will you even remember it?

10 Are things better than they were yesterday? Has the thing bottomed out and is it moving in the right direction? Has the graph turned upwards?

11 Talk to somebody. A problem shared *is* a problem halved. Notice that this could include just writing about the issue in a diary or notebook.

DAY 7

Start now!

CHAPTER 15

Start now!

There are so many ways you could combine the tools you have learnt over the previous six days to come up with a result. I've never seen two people pick exactly the same set of techniques for dealing with their situation. How you go about solving your problems will be unique to you.

Early on I talked you through using your imagination and visualising where you want to be. Be sure not to neglect this very important part of the process. Take some time right now to visualise how your life will be and how you can achieve more in your day and be totally relaxed about it.

Think about the details – getting home from work at a reasonable hour, taking on a new hobby, feeling excited about the week ahead, feeling healthy, calm and in control. Daydream about this – or picture it in bed at night before you go to sleep. Use the checklist in Chapter 2 if that will help you to build this picture. Talk to somebody else about it – a friend, a loved one. Promise yourself some sort of reward – very important this – if you manage to succeed in what you're setting out to do.

> Think about the details – getting home from work at a reasonable hour, taking on a new hobby, feeling excited about the week ahead, feeling healthy, calm and in control. Daydream about this – or picture it in bed at night before you go to sleep.

Below I've listed some ways you might want to use the book after the initial read through you've just done. These aren't prescriptive, but it's just to give you a head start on approaches that have proved to be successful. Have a read through them and think about what works best for you. Whatever you do, as I said in the Introduction, let me know what happens.

Scenario number 1 – Quick wins

You could decide you just wanted to be able to plan for the unplanned and then Chapter 11 would get you doing that. Or you could say that you'd try to get more done by creating extra time in your life. Chapter 12 would get you up and running in that case.

Scenario number 2 – Use the insights from the questionnaires

You could just go to Chapter 13, look at your questionnaire and the places where you scored high and begin doing what the table in Chapter 13 says. Or you could turn to any of Chapters 6, 8 or 9. Look at the questionnaire there and the places where you scored high. If you began to use the particular technique described in that chapter, it would start to make a difference immediately.

Scenario number 3 – Keep your system running

Remember your system. There was the list, appointment tracking, filing and time recording.

1　Start with your list.
2　Prioritise it.
3　Agree your vicious prioritisation priorities with your stakeholders.
4　Generate your list of what has to be done today. Do those things and record where your time goes.

5   When new things come in, add them to the list but only after you have prioritised them – if necessary, talking to the stakeholders.

6   As you start to build up the profile of where your time is going, see whether you're happy with that. If not, take some actions to change it.

7   Repeat steps 4 through 6 until you're happy with the way you're spending your time.

Scenario number 4 – Yet another way

Here's yet another way you could begin to get more done. In what follows I've assumed that somebody's working in a job, in a company or an office or something like that. But if you work in the home, then just replace the phrases like 'before you go home' with 'before you stop for the day' and 'when you come in' with 'when you start'.

Here we go:

1   It's not essential but, if you like, make a note of the average amount of time you spend at work at the moment.

2   This evening, before you go home, derive from your list (i.e. make) a list of all of the things that need to be done tomorrow.

3   Rate them 'A' through 'D' as in Chapter 12. Remember that this is what the letters mean:

●   'A': *I have to get this done today.* Planets will collide, stars will fall, bosses will be grumpy, share prices will nose-dive if this thing isn't done.

●   'B': *It'd be nice to get it done today.*

●   'C': *Realistically, I'm not going to get this done today.*

●   'D': *Delegate it.* I can get somebody else to do this.

4   Tomorrow when you come in, delegate any 'D's you have. When you do this you may want to add a job to your list (for

today, tomorrow or whenever) to go and check that the particular thing was done.

5 Do the 'A's. When you take up an 'A', try as far as is humanly possible not to allow yourself to be interrupted until it's finished.

6 When all the 'A's are done and any 'D's checked on that need to be checked on today, then you're nearly ready to stop or go home. Just one more thing you need to do and that is to put together tomorrow's list. (Come on – it'll only take a minute.) So make the list, 'A', 'B', 'C', 'D'. There you are. Now you can stop (if you're working in the home) or go home (if you work at a place of work).

7 As you do stop or go home, don't feel guilty. If anyone watches you disapprovingly or says anything that indicates that they're unhappy, tell them that you really had a good day today and that you got everything that you needed to do done. Tell them you're trying out a very simple technique and that, based on today's experience, it really seems to have worked. Tell them that if they're interested, you'll explain it to them.

8 Have a great evening.

9 Tomorrow when you come in or start, it'll be back to step 4.

10 Do this for a week and notice the difference. If you want to, calculate how much time you spent at work for this week and compare it with the number at step 1 above.

Scenario number 5 – Working ahead

If, after a week or two, you find that scenario number 4 is working for you – and if you do it religiously, it can't not work – then you could extend it by trying the following. Here it is, right from the top, again.

1 This evening, before you go home, derive from your list (i.e. make) a list of all of the things that need to be done tomorrow.

2   Rate them 'A' through 'D' as in Chapter 12. Remember that this is what the letters mean:

- 'A': *I have to get this done today.* Planets will collide, stars will fall, bosses will be grumpy, share prices will nose-dive if this thing isn't done.

- 'B': *It'd be nice to get it done today.*

- 'C': *Realistically, I'm not going to get this done today.*

- 'D': *Delegate it.* I can get somebody else to do this.

3   Tomorrow when you come in, delegate any 'D's you have. When you do this you may want to add a job to your list (for today, tomorrow or whenever) to go and check that the particular thing was done.

4   Do the 'A's. When you take up an 'A', try as far as is humanly possible not to allow yourself to be interrupted until it's finished.

5   When all the 'A's are done and any 'D's checked on that need to be checked on today, put together tomorrow's list and do the rankings 'A', 'B', 'C', 'D'.

6   Now, instead of stopping or going home, start in on this list, i.e. return to step 3 above. Now you're working ahead. You're doing tomorrow's work today. Stop / go home whenever it suits you. It might be that you get half of tomorrow's work done – or even all of it. Now if somebody looks disapproving, or makes some snide comment, then that's going to be an interesting conversation, when you tell them what you've done now.

7   Before you go home, as always, prepare your list for tomorrow. (The reason I recommend this is twofold. First, you can then put work out of your head for the rest of the day – and the night! Second, in that mysterious way that the subconscious works, you can often find yourself the next

> Before you go home prepare your list for tomorrow.

morning with clearer insights into the things you're planning to do, better ways of doing them, alternative approaches, smarter actions that you can take.)

8   Have a good evening. Forget about work – there's no need to think about it because it's all on your list.

9   In the morning, pick it up at step 3.

Using this technique you could actually find yourself working several days ahead. Then you could think about taking a Friday off!

Notes

1 Dilts, Robert B. *Changing Belief Systems with Neuro-Linguistic Programming* (*NLP*). Capitola, CA: Meta Publications.

2 Dyer, Wayne (1977) *Your Erroneous Zones*. London: Michael Joseph.

3 Jeffreys, Susan (1991) *Feel the Fear and Do It Anyway*. London: Arrow Books.

4 Ibid.

5 O'Connell, Fergus (2007) *Fast Projects: Project Management When Time Is Short*. Harlow, UK: Prentice Hall.

6 Dyer (1977).

7 Ibid.

8 Ibid.

9 Ibid.